Developing Your

SIXTH SENSE

Developing Your

SIXTH SENSE

Master Your Awareness for Greater Clarity, Wisdom and Power

STUART WILDE

MEDIA

Published 2022 by Gildan Media LLC
aka G&D Media
www.GandDmedia.com

FIRST EDITION 2022

Front cover design by David Rheinhardt of Pyrographx

Interior design by Meghan Day Healey of Story Horse, LLC

Library of Congress Cataloging-in-Publication Data is available upon request

ISBN: 978-1-7225-0591-2

10 9 8 7 6 5 4 3 2 1

Contents

1

Dimensions of Profound Awareness

You have to apply the power of a higher awareness
in your life to reap the rewards of success.

Developing your sixth sense is much more than the process of enhancing or bringing forward your awareness and psychic ability. That's what's so exciting about the material in this book as we go through the steps together, chapter by chapter.

What is the sixth sense? The sixth sense is a sacred energy—a cosmic state of inner knowing. And with that inner knowing comes a special power hand-in-hand with a higher state of consciousness and a greater spiritual awareness. That is why we seek to develop our sixth sense, in order to make a greater connection with the infinite self and the eternal light within.

The process is one of shining a light on our evolution as humans, empowering us with an esoteric inner power, a special power, one that was used by the initiates of old who knew how to access the ancient wisdoms, the chakras, and the etheric web. *Etheric* relates to the heavens or spiritual world.

The process of unlocking the sixth sense is sacred and special. It changes you for the better and gives you more energy to draw from, and that is what makes the time and effort that you spend on developing your sixth sense worthwhile. I see the sixth sense as a dimension of awareness. It's like stepping through a doorway to another place. Once you pass through, your life changes, you move to a more special evolution in this lifetime, one that is higher than where you find yourself right now.

The transition comes about when you see yourself in a sacred way as vastly more than just a physical body, when you see that you are ready to move to a higher ground, that you do genuinely desire, to reach beyond the mundane to a special level of spirituality, because you are more than just a physical body, so you can perceive more than just the physical world.

It seems to me that the level of your awareness and the acuteness of your sixth-sense perception is inexorably linked with the quality of your life's journey. The Russian philosopher George Gurdjieff talked a lot about the *sleeping man*, which was a term he used to describe the consciousness of a bourgeois mundane life. Gurdjieff said that one is required to exercise the force of will in order to wake oneself up in this lifetime. Otherwise, one drifts through life more or less in a sleep state, missing most of the good stuff.

I must say watching people coming out of a subway trotting off to work or heading down the freeway in the rush hour, you can see the kind of collective sleep state that Gurdjieff was talking about.

If you've ever had the experience of finding that time has flown by in, say, a week or a month or a year, without your really being aware of it, then you've slipped into Gurdjieff's sleeping man state. In the sleep state, time flies; conversely, in the spiritually awake sixth-sense state, time slows down and reality gets thicker. By thicker I don't mean it's heavier, or more negative or harder to move through. What I mean is time becomes richer; you're aware of more; your timeframes are broader and your vista is more expansive.

If you've ever listened to a record after taking a puff or two of the wacky baccy, you'll know how suddenly your feelings open up and you've heard loads more of the tune or the song than you thought.

It is my intention for this book to do much the same. To open you up because these concepts open up the energy centers in your subtle body. You naturally go from stiff to pliant, from resistant to fluid, from hesitant to flowing. Once you open up to your higher power and inner knowing, you won't need any mind-altering substances to perceive life in all its subtlety and vastness.

In fact, although drugs may create an altered state of consciousness, they destroy your subtle energy, the etheric, and though you may experience a momentary gain of perception, by using drugs, long term, you will become duller, less perceptive, and more open to danger.

The sixth sense takes discipline to exercise the force of will, which you know from personal experience is very strong. You can engage your sixth sense in a negative, destructive way, or you can use it positively to wake yourself up. Sometimes, of course, the universe configures a wake-up call for you, and something weird happens and life whacks you in the head or wakes you up that way. But this awareness I am talking about in this book is better, as it saves you having to go through any nasty shocks. But the very fact that you feel you need to develop the sixth sense says you have the courage, discipline, and follow through to enliven your consciousness, and that's a marvelous thing.

You want to reach to a higher state of awareness, a higher metaphysical ability, a higher spirituality inside a more profound sense of self. That is the reason for your journey in this lifetime. In the chapters ahead, with the various tools, techniques, and disciplines that I'll be sharing with you, you will see that the process requires a certain amount of concentration and dedication.

You have to apply the power of a higher awareness in your life to reap the rewards of success. That awareness comes in the form of ESP, an extrasensory perception, which comes from allowing reality to impact your subtle body, and allowing that impact to register as energy perception in your mind. It grants you a multifaceted awareness of what is going on around you. For example, in your relationships, when you start to become aware of the subtle or subliminal information that flows from you toward others, as well as energy and emotions that flow from others to you, you realize that you can pick up on what others are thinking, and you'll become more aware, relationships improve, you'll attract a higher quality of person. You can use the same awareness, that sixth sense, in financial matters and business. Perceptions will carry you not only to where financial opportunities lie, but they will help you to avoid suffering financial losses, which I discuss later.

The process is one of tapping back into that reservoir of ideas and creativity that lie hidden deep within you. One half-decent idea can make you a million dollars. And there are lots of people out there who have come up with an idea, or in a vision, or in a dream or meditation or as a flash of inspiration, and that idea has made them wealthy for life.

The idea doesn't have to be particularly radical. In fact, more often than not successful ideas aren't outlandish at all because they have to be easily accepted and understood by people in the marketplace. Expressing an original idea or developing a concept, product, or service in a creative way is often all that it takes, and the fact that you can do it is not particularly difficult.

So in developing a higher awareness, you get more in touch with your relationships, your finance, and your creative expression. As you become more aware, and more at peace with yourself, you develop more confidence around you, which automatically brings out your skills. In fact, you may suddenly realize, *Wow, I have all these abilities that I've never really understood before, or I wasn't aware of. I'll pull them out and dust them off and sell them to someone in some way or other.*

Or perhaps you are aware of your ability, but you've never been confident enough to express who you really are before. So the journey toward the sixth sense is wider, larger, and bigger than just party tricks, fortune-telling, and the ability to read tarot cards. It's really a part of your heritage, your spiritual journey in this lifetime.

You may describe that journey in whatever spiritual or religious or sacred terms that you wish. In the end, the sixth sense is energy, and that energy can direct you toward a greater, more colorful inner self, which reflects a more enriched outer self. Life when you look at it is a replica, an external manifestation of your thoughts and feelings. When things happen that you don't understand, or when things fail to happen that you feel ought to happen, you are confused because whatever you are expecting in your life hasn't shown up. There is always an explanation.

It's explicable somewhere in the deepest, most subtle feelings and thoughts that lie hidden within the subconscious mind, within the impulses and motivations that are hidden there. Below the threshold of normal waking perception, there's always an answer in there somewhere.

By getting in touch with your intuition—shall we call it your psychic ability, your sixth sense—and I'm going to define these terms for you very specifically, what you're really doing is giving notice to that spiritual infinite part of you. You're saying, *Hey, I want to know more, I want to see more, I want to understand.*

Rather than being a victim of circumstances, being someone who's just carried along, one who allows life to happen to them, you are saying, instead, I want to generate my life. I want to control my life and my destiny. I want to exert the force of my will upon my destiny so that life gives me those things that I'm entitled to.

Think of it like this: Imagine if through some magical power, you could know everything that there was to know on this Earth. Instantly, you would become the most powerful person in the world because of the level of your knowledge. You would know what everybody was thinking, how everybody's destiny was about to unfold, how the stock market was going to perform, which horse was going to win the next race at Santa Anita. You'd become immensely powerful and very, very rich.

The opposite of that is this: Imagine you know nothing. If you couldn't remember your name, you didn't know where you lived, what day of the week it was, you had no idea how to buy food, how to maintain yourself, you would be powerless.

Therefore, somewhere between knowing everything and nothing is where human consciousness lies. It's where our evolution orbits. If you develop and tap into the sixth sense, you begin to tap into knowledge, you gain personal power, and life becomes less fearful. You gradually exit a mundane evolution and step up to a higher ground. You go beyond the karma of day-to-day reality to a safer plane of existence.

Perception takes you from relative powerlessness to real strength and real knowledge. And that's what I really mean by personal power. Physical power, physical strength, political strength, and social clout are all fleeting. Physical power wanes, political parties come and go, today's glamour pose is tomorrow's has-been.

Real energy is indestructible. Real knowledge is perpetual. That's what we're looking for here. We're looking to the immense power and value of perception.

Over a period of the last several hundred years, humanity has developed greatly, and as our societies have become cleverer and more reliant upon the intellect, we have become so intellectually focused that any process that is not logical or information that is not logically arrived at and that does not conform to the Newtonian ideas of being mechanically explicable—this subtle information is derided and ridiculed as being faulty, random, or fanciful.

Yet everyone has had sixth-sense experiences, strange happenings, psychic intuitive moments. I'm sure you have as well. A moment before the phone rang, you heard someone's name in your head, or you thought about a distant relative, and suddenly they call. We were all given an intuitive sixth sense, and we should make use of our God-given gifts. Why would we get any more gifts if we haven't used the ones we have already been given?

Training your sixth sense is a good thing; it opens you up and makes you ready for even greater things. I believe that at a deep inner subconscious level—what Carl Jung would call the collective unconscious—we are all linked. There is no space-time difference in consciousness. We are as close to somebody who is 10,000 miles away as we are to the person next to us, or the child in arms, or even to someone who has made the transition from the Earth plane.

In the realm of consciousness, we're all linked. So I'll be talking about how to spatially shrink the planet, how to bring everything and everyone closer to you, or to push them away when you don't want them near you. Once you are outside the normal space-time continuum in the world of the inner self, you can shift the shape of reality around you to suit your needs.

In the end, the idea that things are fixed is part of the illusion of the physical plane. They are and they aren't. The fact that our intellectual thinkers, professors, and writers have ridiculed these esoteric ideas has, in fact, been a great disservice to humankind. It has cut us off from a natural perception, from a higher flow. Logic, science, medicine, and research have greatly assisted our evolution as human beings on this planet, but our interconnectedness and perception is also vital.

Here's something interesting to think about. I doubt that there's a single self-made millionaire on the planet who didn't use their sixth sense in order to make those millions. Every scientist uses the sixth sense to work out their formulas and ideas. We all use it but many can't admit to it. A lot of sixth-sense perception is the ability to imagine and intuit new ideas from old ones. For example, you could be writing a piece of music, and just plunking along with a few notes. And you might think that sounds like it might have commercial appeal. At that point, you don't know that it's going to sell 11 million copies. It's an intuitive guess, but you put it down on your music sheet because the notes feel right.

Everything has energy—the marketplace of life, relationships, money, products, your actions, creativity, music—it's all energy. And so you can pluck information about that energy via the subtle senses. You might meet a man or woman who might be exactly the opposite of what your intellect thought you'd be attracted to. They're tall and skinny with a big nose, and you were expecting someone of average height and musculature with a perfectly shaped nose. They may not be the same culture, nationality, or religion that you were expecting, but there's something about them. It's a feeling about their energy, and, suddenly, you know there's your special mate in this lifetime.

As we enter the realm of the sixth sense, start to make the concept right, immediately. Understand that it isn't woo-woo; whatever is happening is part of a sacred journey. It's the ability to operate outside the world of the intellect.

The sixth sense is a part of brain function. It has to come to you as fleeting impressions, thoughts, and feelings—a logic that is illogical. People don't understand it. But as you understand it, you'll find it sets you free. Some worry about being criticized and ridiculed. And of course, you don't want people thinking you're a complete space cadet. The answer to these worries is this: Don't tell people what you're doing. You're on a sacred journey. It's silent, it's special, and you don't have to tell the whole neighborhood because they won't understand for the most part.

I must say these subtle energies have helped me a lot in my lifetime because, as I develop more and more inner knowing, life offered up its secrets. I'd be walking down the street, and I'd look at a person and much of their life story would evolve in front of my eyes. I'd know them. If I then had to prove my perception, it would be lost. It's much too subtle. So why bother discussing it or defending the illogical?

Remember, this journey is about more than just psychic powers. It's the story of your spiritual journey on the Earth plane. It's the epic grandeur of your life, the evolution of your consciousness. It's a step from the tick-tock consciousness of the intellectual mundane world to a higher consciousness in the realm of the gods, in the realm of a greater spirituality.

A Return to Natural Spirituality

Moving from the idea of the sixth sense being a part of your spiritual heritage, a part of your connectedness to all things, a part of your sacred journey, we need to look now at what it actually is. In other words, what benefits will the sixth sense bring you and how do you reclaim it? As we get into the nitty gritty, let me go over some important main points.

One of the reasons why this inner knowing doesn't come to us easily anymore is because we moved out of our tribal natural state into the intellectual financial competitive state. The nature of our evolution has changed. In the olden days, people aligned to the elements. In other words, they had an etheric connection to fire, earth, air, and water. And so they were connected to the atavistic or ancient spirit of nature, and the spirit and vitality of their tribe and its tribal knowledge or memory.

Just as birds know when there's going to be an earthquake, because they can feel the electromagnetic changes and the subtle shifts of energy as pressure drops, so in ancient times, the tribal people used the same inner knowing, that sense of connectedness. They listened to what nature had to say to them, so they could keep themselves safe. Obviously, once we develop knowledge, science, and intellect, the inner knowing atrophied and died because it wasn't quite so important. You could calculate when the crops were going to grow using a computer; you didn't just have to feel the time was right. You could plot the height of the rivers and where they would flow by satellite and so on.

Your inner sense has died somewhat. Therefore, the first process in taking you back to this natural spirituality is getting you in touch with your nature self. It's important to remember even if you are a confirmed city dweller, you are the wind, you are the fire of the sun, you are the water in the air, you are the etheric, the life force, the animals. We're all made of very ancient stardust, and our components all came from the same galactic place.

When you're out in nature or when you have time to stop and contemplate, see bands of energy coming up through the Earth, through your body, and feel those bands of energy going out from you to the animal kingdom, to the minerals, to the plant kingdom, and beyond to all the humans evolving on this planet.

Take a moment to visualize this current season and then move your mind through all the other seasons that will follow during the year. Feel yourself aligned to the subtle shifts that take place as the sun moves from the north to the south and back again. And as you align to the seasons, be aware of your position on this planet and its position among the stars. And think of the Earth at your feet, feel grounded, and think about the stars above you and our position in the solar system. Embracing the nature self is the act of placing yourself geographically in a finite body on Mother Earth, while developing your consciousness in an infinite dimension.

Action Step: As your first discipline, say this to your-self regularly each day: *I am the wind, the fire, the earth, and the water. I am the etheric, I'm aligned to the natu-ral laws and all the information they contain.* Make this your mantra, and within a week or two of aligning your consciousness to nature, a subtle shift takes place. If you can, try to spend time outdoors on your own. Go to the mountains, sleep there on the ground, embrace the natural ebb and flow of things. Go on your own and quiet your mind and remain silent. Turn within and claim back your natural humanity and the simplicity of your nature self. It awaits.

The next simple step toward the sixth sense is to train yourself to notice things. The mind is lazy. It has trained itself to ignore everything except those things that please it. By forcing the mind to notice things, you engage it. You're telling it that you want to be aware of life and that you want to claim back what has been lost. By training yourself to notice things, you activate the five senses, and you stimulate perception and reactivate your main sense, which, of course, is that of subtle feeling.

In addition, by stopping to notice, you place your-self more firmly inside this incarnation as a human, while you move out of your head and into your heart. In other words, you're not letting life just wash past you. If life washes past you, a day becomes a week, a week a month, a month year, and suddenly you're old and gray and dead. But by stopping to notice, you are requiring the mind to come back from its world, its needs and its pleasures, and to enter your world, the human world.

Action Step: Start to notice small details, they are important. If you're at home right now, stop to notice the room you're in. How many lights? Are all the lights working? If you're in the bath, count the tiles so you know, yes, you will say there are 132 white tiles in my bathroom, and three are cracked.

Now think of a street that you go down regularly. Write down everything that you can remember about that street. Most likely, you'll discover that you can't remember very much. And the pizza shop that you thought was on the corner is in fact two shops down. Though you've been up and down the street a thousand times, you won't remember the half of it.

Then go to the street and fill in the missing bits. Write down everything you see. What do the traffic signs say? How long is the street? What parking regulations are enforced? What are the main features of the street, the shape, the size, the shops, and so on? If there's graffiti on the wall on the corner, what does it say? What color are the shop fronts? Which shop is next to which other shop?

Write down a detailed map and description of your street and remember it and then wait a few days and have a friend test you. If you make any mistakes, go back to the street as many times as it takes until you accurately remember everything. Let your mind know that you won't let it off the hook until it can remember each and everything that there is to know in your selected street.

It doesn't matter if this exercise takes a month and you have to go back twelve times. What you're saying is, detail is important. The effort is worthwhile. Make it a discipline to take stock of your situation every time you find yourself somewhere new.

Let's say you're visiting an office today. You haven't been there before. As you walk in, pause, cast your eyes left and right, up and down. How does the office feel? What is your first and overriding impression? What's the feeling here: happiness, anger, boredom, indifference? The office will be laced, painted if you like, with people's emotions and their thinking. What can your inner knowing tell you about this office that you're just walking into?

Now, start counting stuff. How many people are there? How many desks? What color are the blinds? Are the filing cabinets gray, black, or some other color? Try to pick up all that general information with just one or two casts of your eyes.

Make a mental picture of the office in your mind's eye. And while you're waiting for your appointment, run through the mental picture, enhancing it and remembering it. Remember the picture the room makes in your mind. Don't try to remember the actual room. The picture can last for hours, days, or years, even though your physical presence in the room may be short.

Action Step: Do this. Take a deck of cards and turn over three cards as fast as you can flip your hand over and let the cards make a mental picture in your mind, pause, then turn over three more. And then three more again. Run through three sets of three, so nine cards in total. Now go back to the mental picture, your memory of the mental picture, that you had of the first set of three. What were the cards? And the second set of three? What was in the third set of three? Don't bother trying to remember the actual cards. Just close your eyes and ask your mind to give you the three mental pictures.

I used to teach blackjack courses to people who wanted to make a living at the game. When you're playing blackjack, you don't have time to count cards in real time, as a croupier moves them from your vision as fast as he or she can. So the way to become a blackjack pro is to remember the pictures that a group of cards make in your head. No croupier in the world can move faster than the speed of light. And that is the speed at which the picture comes to you as light comes off the cards to your eye.

People would ask me if I ever got intimidated in the casino by fast dealers. And I'd tell them fast dealers are good; hands come to you more quickly, and the more hands you have, the more profit you make. Most people don't realize that speed doesn't make a difference to a professional player. How fast the dealer deals, it doesn't matter. The pro remembers the mind pictures, not the cards. So the more hands that have been dealt, the more money the professional player makes.

Remember, there's a subtle difference between reality, as it is in the real world, and the pictures of reality that reflected light sends back to your mind. Reality changes, but the pictures stay. It's only a matter of telling your mind to hold onto the pictures. Eventually, you'll be able to remember cards you saw a month ago.

When you do the card exercise, if at first you find three cards too hard to remember, then turn over sets of just two cards, or even one card at a time. Once you've got this part down pat, try more cards, expand your perception, try flipping over sets of four or even six cards, wait a few seconds, and see if you can accurately describe all six cards you saw and the positions you saw them in from left to right. Don't be daunted; you're only remembering the image, the knock that the light makes in your mind's eye.

Eventually, you get so fast in your ability to notice, you'll be able to pick up cards, or the details of a room, in a split second, hardly moving your eyes. Noticing is fun. It gives you a sense of power. And it instantly shows you things you never saw before.

Think of this, if you lived eighty years, and you slept for a third of that, you're left with fifty-six years in the waking state. Now if you only notice, say 25 percent of life, your fifty-six waking years come down to a real lifespan or a real perception of just fourteen years. So imagine fourteen years in relation to the eighty that you are alive on this Earth plane and how much of those fourteen years you'll be mentally talking to yourself. And much of your life will be spent doing ordinary tasks like bathing, mopping the floor, and hauling the kids to school.

In the end, your life might come down to fewer than six to eight real years of quality, conscious, awake, valuable action. Six to eight years of noticing life, time in which you experienced your humanity in its real definition. That's very sad, isn't it?

Life passes most people by. They're asleep or day-dreaming in their heads. Copious thinking is the disease of the egocentric; it's their escape mechanism so they can avoid real life. There is only one way to transcend life, and that is going through it, not avoiding it or going round it. You raise your energy and you go beyond things by experiencing them. Understanding what happened, reconciling it all, and moving on. Through is the only way that works. And it is by moving through life you develop confidence, power, awareness, and the sixth sense.

The sixth sense divides up into three main categories and several subcategories. They are the intuitive sixth sense, the psychic sixth sense—these two are slightly different. I'll explain later. Then there's the all-knowing sixth sense, the sensuality of the sixth sense, the auditory sixth sense—which are sixth-sense perceptions that come to you through hearing—and the visionary sixth sense. I'll go through all of these definitions, and I'll show you how to access them.

Each forms a vital part of your journey to a higher consciousness, and each is reliant on developing your subtle body, the etheric. I'll talk about the subtle body at length, and I'll teach you how to develop it with simple exercises and spiritual strengthening, and we'll discuss the chakras. I'll give you some simple exercises, so that you can discover the etheric energy centers, the chakras in your own body. By the end of this book, you will know how to activate your energy correctly. You'll begin to feel the power centers in your subtle body, and you'll understand what they mean and what they're telling you.

Activating your energy will allow more vitality to come into your being. It enlivens you and heals you. Next, I will discuss how you will develop your five senses so you can access the various categories of heightened awareness and the sixth sense. I'll show you how you can, simply and easily with just a little bit of discipline and concentration and with some simple exercises, step into a power that will eventually become an unlimited source of joy and strength and wonder for you.

2

Heightening the Five Senses for Greater Perception

*Getting the five senses acute
is how the sixth sense develops.*

Generally, you can't really notice life until you get out of the tendency of being obsessed with self. Our modern societies, because of the media, train people to become unreasonably self-indulgent and self-centered.

Now it's good to look after yourself and honor yourself and to concentrate on your life. But there is a fine line between what is reasonable and the way most people operate. If the only thoughts going off in your head start with *I this* and *I that*, then the ego has you in its grip, and it will gradually shrink your personal world to where its whims and neuroses are all that you ever see.

The ego is much like a small child who makes a huge fuss creating a scene so that its mother would attend to it and put aside whatever she is doing to care for the child. People spend their lives mentally preening themselves and constantly thinking and talking about themselves, and so they can't properly hear or perceive. And when others talk, they don't listen or they are listening to the incessant chatter of their ego personality droning on in their head. So they have very little ability to perceive what is outside of them. They walk up the street or meet a friend and share a meal, and several hours of life have gone by without them seeing or hearing anything other than themselves.

An obsession with self collapses your universe to a tiny place where your focus just on self and the outpourings of what is often a fearful and disconnected mind. You miss most of what is going on, and life becomes a blur. Most people can't describe what happened yesterday, never mind last week. People resting solely inside of themselves and their ideas have a one-sided view of the human experience. They have no frame of reference in which to comprehend the greater picture, and they have no solid framework outside of self.

In the perpetual mutterings of the ego, you have no real connection to your inner self and the sixth sense either. So as you begin to open up and become more aware, you will discipline the mind away from itself and toward others and life. When the mind chatters to you, stop it by saying, *I don't need to think about that now. I will deal with these concerns later.* Alternatively, as it speaks, say, *I don't accept that energy. I am serene and silent.* Then take a moment to notice something outside of you, stare at the ant that's climbing up the garden gate, look at a high building and stare at the way the bricks on the third floor join into those that make up the fourth floor. Notice everything that there is to notice about those bricks.

In other words, you are looking to move your focus away from the ego personality's chatter to a more silent mind that is focused on perceiving energy and perceiving the subtleties of life. You are gradually stepping to a more valuable spiritual infinite view of self and a more full view in human terms. Information begins to flow toward you rather than past you.

Action Step: So for the next twenty-four hours, every time your mind starts to talk to you and if that dialogue begins with the *I* word—*I think this, I want that*—stop it. Instead of engaging the mind with talking about self, occupy it with the act of noticing something. Such practice is a good discipline, and it strengthens your force of will.

Let's talk about developing the five senses, which is the fastest and simplest way of opening yourself up to the sixth sense. As we go through the five senses, I will give you some useful ideas to mull over.

The first step is to crank up your awareness of your sense of **sight**. If you are not blind, you probably take this sense for granted. As humans we don't have to make an effort to see, but we do have to make an effort to notice, as I have been discussing. As a discipline, take a little notebook with you as you go through the day. Make a note of things that you see. It doesn't matter if what you see is unusual or not. Just write down events, people, and actions that have taken place in front of you.

In writing a journal of what you see, you take the mind further away from itself, and you make being here in the now important, and you are also affirming that all information is valuable to you. You are prepared to make the effort to gather even the most innocuous bits of information. Later you will refine your instructions to the mind so it cuts out the mundane and clicks in quickly when there is a special sign or when something unusual is going on. But for now, instruct your mind that you want to notice and remember everything, however humdrum.

Training your mind to really see in the external world will stimulate your will, because you will be forcing the mind to put aside itself to heed your wishes. By disempowering the ego's neurotic world, you liberate and empower yourself to dream a big dream; you can materialize a big vision for yourself. You will stretch beyond to greater possibilities. This enlargement of your greater vision is vital in the development of the sixth sense.

Action Step: Wait for starry night. Start by finding all the main constellations. If you don't already know them, perhaps you could start with your birth sign. It's fun to know where your stars are. Eighty-eight constellations are recognized by astronomers. Of course, they won't all be in your patch of the sky at any one time, but at least learn to pick out the main ones; the rest will come later.

Learning the sky is a spiritual exercise. It gives you a whole bunch of new friends and enlarges you, but, most of all, knowing the sky gives you a geography. You place yourself beyond the ego's myopic world into a greater world of light years and enormous distances and vast masses. By knowing the stars, you place yourself in your proper context—inside an evolution that is universal and infinite.

I can't stress how important this is, for the visionary is not a victim of his or her mind. They control it. They are larger than life, eternal, beyond death. Do this, pause for a moment, and remember that you are eternal, spread across a vast age, straddling across both past and future. And in this grand mindset, spread yourself out, cast your thoughts to a distant future, and think about people, perhaps those who will be living here on the very ground you stand on right now, 500 years from now. Pause to reflect who they might be and what their hopes and dreams might contain and how perhaps you could help them and strengthen them and wish them well.

For the future, though it has not yet formed, exists in its virtual spiritual state right now. So breathe in a long breath, and as you exhale, send love via your breath to your countrymen and women, those who are here right now and those who might be alive on this very same day of the year, in this very place 500 years in the future. As you breathe out, feel yourself projecting light into the future, place your positive energy forward in time. Be yourself a part of that future epoch or via the eternity within you, you will be there in a kind of way. Of course, a small part of you will be there via the record of your memories, those that you have placed by your thoughts and actions into the global mind, which is the perpetual record of the evolution of humanity to which you belong. You are an eternal being in a physical form. Thinking about the distant future and sending it energy helps you straddle across time, in an eternal stance.

As I said, once you know the sky and the stars, you will find that they become your friends, and you will know better where *you* are. If you seek direction in life, knowing where you are is the first step. It seems odd to me that so many seek direction in the sense that they want a break or they need someone to help them or they seek a path to follow. But if you ask them what direction they are facing right now in the physical sense, they can't tell north from south. Their lack of relationship to the physical planet and their position in the universe doesn't say much for their sense of direction.

If you want direction in life, start working out where you are right now and make a mental note from time to time during the day. Ask: *Where am I? How far from where? How close to what? Am I facing north or south? Do I have my head tucked in the sand like so many others? Or do I know where I am going?* Knowing where you are in relation to things is an affirmation that says, *I am not helpless and lost and self-obsessed. I know where I am. And I am moving forward from here in a northward direction, seventeen miles from downtown, and I stand in an eternal stance in a galactic place.* Sight is more than just looking at things; it is also positioning yourself geographically in relation to things.

While gazing up at the night sky, pick a spot that is black and seemingly starless. Stare at that dark spot and pull it to you in your feelings. And bit by bit you will see stars that were not there a few minutes ago. Buy a pair of binoculars and then look up and you will see thousands of stars and galaxies made up of billions of stars, many of them like our own Sun, and they have planets like ours orbiting them and things are happening up there. The stars you see above you at night are all part of the Milky Way, our home. But beyond that is the fuzzy haze of some of the twelve nearby galaxies and beyond them a billion more. It is a very big playground we find ourselves in, very big. Awesome really.

The other direction in which you will need to crank up your site is inward through dreams and visions and meditations. But before I discuss that subject, let's go on to the sense of **hearing**. All the dreams and visions in the world won't help you much, if you don't know the finer, more subtle points of listening, which I am sure you will have guessed by now is more than just cocking your ear in the direction of noise.

Hearing is vital for, in its greater definition, is comprehension. Most people are confused about life, and they don't understand it. And they can't understand people, and they don't comprehend much of what is going on. They may hear very well, but it doesn't help them as they haven't mastered comprehension. Of course, often they can't be bothered to engage the concentration that it takes to comprehend. They find it easier to remain unaware. But if you engage your concentration and you develop the discipline necessary, you can walk out of the fog of a cloudy life into clarity and perception.

Generally, we train our minds to block out most incoming sounds, because they are irrelevant—traffic noise, kids screaming, the radio playing, that kind of stuff. However, you will change that and you will demand that the mind listen carefully. So you will learn to search for noises, and you will ask what it means and you will learn to listen. It's easy.

Making the mind concentrate in this way disciplines it. You are now taking a different attitude to hearing, you are affirming your desire for awareness, and you affirm that you are a spiritual being who is prepared to focus internally and listen to the subtle inner messages, as well as to the world outside of you. You are saying, *I will listen to the world around me and, in the act of noticing its sounds, I will become more aware of the subtle promptings of my heart. I will hear the voice of spirit within me. I am affirming by this action that I am prepared to listen to the promptings of spirit.*

Remember, deafness is the inability of a man or a woman to hear their heart. If you can't listen to your heart, you are truly deaf, regardless of how good your hearing is. Of course, in this context, I mean listening to your heart in the sense of the promptings of spirit.

Action Step: As an affirmation, listen to the subtle promptings of your heart. To do this, place your finger on your pulse several times a day. As you hear your heart beating, pause to think about the spaces between the beats; focus your concentration on them. The pauses are what death sounds like. Now shift your concentration onto the beat. And that's what life sounds like. And as you listen to the pulse, tell your heart that you are prepared to listen and act on its subtle promptings. If you look after your heart, you will enhance your hearing ability.

Also, try this, sit on a park bench, close your eyes, and relax. Start by just listening to what is going on around you—listen to conversations, hear life, its animation, its liveliness, its grand emotion. Sound is all around you.

Now begin stretching your hearing by reaching past what is normally audible and visualize yourself with huge, ultra-sensitive elf-like ears, and imagine them on a rotational mount so you can turn your big ears 360 degrees in every direction. Tell yourself your hearing has become superdirectional. You can now move your ears and search for sounds. Focus on a faint sound in the distance, then ask your mind's auditory capacity to bring that sound closer to you. Pull it to you, and it will get louder. It doesn't matter if you can't hear it clearly; it is just the act of concentrating on the sound that matters. It is kind of funny because in visualizing big ears, you can actually improve your hearing.

You may also want to cup one of your hands behind one ear and then take the other hand and cup it in front of the opposite ear. That way you heighten your hearing backward with one ear and forward with the other ear.

Now you have created an even more multidirectional sense of hearing, and suddenly you are bigger in your perception through the gift of hearing. To hear well in life, you have to stop your thoughts and control them and eliminate many of them. And you will have to comprehend and perceive.

Action Step: Pick a piece of music you know well. Listen to it as you sit in a chair. Blank your mind and go through the piece listening not just to its overall melody, but try to individualize each and every instrument. Try to really hear the feelings the musicians are putting across as they are playing, to get a sense of the real person and his or her feelings. That's where subtle hearing lies.

Another exercise for empowering your hearing and comprehension is this: Next time you are in a face-to-face conversation with someone, focus your eyes on the tip of their nose and concentrate on it, not moving your eyes, and listen carefully to every word they say. Don't let your mind wander. Listen to the silence between their words, the sighs, and the poignant pauses. Listen to the inflection of their voice as it rises and falls. From time to time move your concentration from the tip of their nose without moving your eyes, watch their pupils and see how they open and shut slightly as they talk. There is understanding to be had.

As you concentrate on your listening ability, search for the subtle feeling behind what is being said. When people talk, most of the information they impart is in their feelings. The words they utter are only a code that describes a thought and that is just an electrical outcropping of an emotion or a subtle feeling. In listening to conversations in this way, you practice focusing, and you become aware of subtle information, and you open yourself up to clairvoyance. It is another way of entering more deeply into the experience of life. Listening is an affirmation. Remember, as a visionary, everything is important to you.

I will deal with the auditory sixth sense in a later chapter, but for right now, practice blanking your mind and accepting more information by using your hearing. Remember, getting the five senses acute is how the sixth sense develops.

Let's move on to the sense of **touch**. Quite often gifted psychics can pick up a lot of information by touching objects. You can give a psychic an item of clothing of a person who has been murdered, and he or she can pick up on the energy of that person and the circumstances of their demise. How do psychics do that? I believe we impact our physical reality with our spiritual metaphysical identity, our subtle energy, and also with our emotions and feelings. There is a theory that says that sound striking a physical object leaves an impact or memory of that impact at a subatomic level. Hypothetically, then, you could strip off the wall in your living room, and there would be a record of everything you have ever said and every TV show you have ever watched, God forbid. Still, aside from that, I feel your subtle energy, emotions, and thinking probably act much like sound impacting reality at a subtle level.

In the end, it is all energy—subatomic, atomic, metaphysical, or something else. It is perpetual in its way. Yes, I am sure there is a perpetual memory that lives on in a record of the universe's evolution if you like.

But consider how will you expand your sensitivity to energy via the sense of touch. One way is to be more aware of the texture and nature of life, embracing its softness and sensuality. This is particularly important for men who tend to abandon their sensitivity for wealth, status, and competition. Men live in a world that is too hard and insensitive, and that hurts them in the end and makes them sad when they burn out with a garage full of stuff that gives them little real pleasure.

While they could have experienced much sensitivity and love, and in doing that, they would have become a bigger energy spiritually, they would have been less hard on themselves, and they would have experienced more goodness and pleasure. Being connected to the real things of life is so much more valuable than the biff-bang world of the modern male.

So much of the sensitivity of both males and females is lost in the madcap rush for status and wealth. The idea that acquisitions will make you happy is a big letdown for most, and eventually the plastic-electronic nature of modern living destroys our sensitivity and much of our real perception of life. So be in touch, notice the feel of things around you, touch a piece of satin or silk and feel its lushness, feel the breeze on your cheeks as you walk in the park, take your shoes off and walk on the earth, feel the soil, the dampness, and note the way this marvelous planet feels under your feet.

Action Step: Pick an evening when you know you will be home alone and blindfold yourself. Now I am presuming here that you are not already visually impaired. If you are, you can skip this one as you will know it through and through. If you are not blind, spend three hours with a blindfold on: fix dinner, do household chores, walk around, listen to the TV if you like. But spend the evening in the realm of touch, and you will be amazed.

At first you will operate a bit spastically and you might become frustrated and irritable. But soon your confidence grows. You will be able to feel your way along and know where things are, especially things that are alive like plants and your pets. They emanate heaps of energy. You just have to focus on picking up that energy more and more.

On this very special blindfolded evening, feel your way along. Reclaim the ability you had as a baby when you touched things, and licked them and fondled them to understand and learn about them. I would not bother licking the cat if I were you. Claim back your sense of touch. It will help your sensitivity, and you'll develop gratefulness for your sight. And that is part of understanding compassion and love. Is it not?

We used to do a variation of this exercise in my men's seminars. I take the men to the edge of a wood, usually one that was rather hilly, and I would blindfold them, and I would make them walk through the wood feeling their way along. Each man was given two eggs to carry, which they were not allowed to break. The eggs signified a man's responsibilities in life—his job, children, family, and so on. Also, the eggs stop the men from blustering through the wood macho style.

For the first five or ten minutes, the men would whack their heads on branches, often falling over. After a bit, they found that if they retired their thinking and engaged their feelings, they would know where the trees were, and the low-hanging branches as well.

Soon they could walk through the woods at almost a normal pace. In this exercise, they had to follow a drumbeat. And often if the drummer who was a staff member not blindfolded was not on his toes or dozed off, the blindfolded men would catch up to him at high speed, and the drummer would have to duck away quickly. I have seen blindfolded men get almost to a slow running speed crouched over, holding their eggs, and feeling out the positions of trees and branches, moving through them at high speed. It was amazing to watch.

After you have done the home-alone blindfolded exercise, go to the woods and try the egg routine there. Take a friend to help you stay safe, so that you don't drop over a cliff or wander out onto a forest road where traffic might pass. Perhaps you could have a go and talk about it and then your friend might try it.

Then again, you can practice anytime in the park or walking down the street. Take a moment to close your eyes and feel where you are. With your eyes shut, try to feel people passing you by—not just their presence, but the overall feeling or energy they emit. You will be astonished how fast your perception grows.

Soon you will be more aware of your surroundings and be able to recognize slight temperature shifts and air pressure changes. You will have trained yourself to feel energy. Try to work out when it will rain next. Use your feelings to detect the change in air pressure as a low front moves through your area, bringing with it rain, and you will notice hours and days in advance. The pressure change is very noticeable.

Reading people's emotions is not a lot different from noticing the air pressure. Even people's most subtle mood swings will impact you and tell you things. I am sure you have experienced entering a room just after people have had a heated argument. You can feel the residue of their antagonism and the emotional or verbal violence. You can feel it in the empty room. It's not an illusion; the energy is there to be felt and understood.

As you begin to develop sensitivity to touch and feeling, you will become more central. Life is more fun. In fact, all of inner knowing in the end is feeling for the most part, isn't it?

As a part of developing sensuality, you can work on your sense of **smell**. You may want to invest in a range of essential oils and take the time to really smell each one so that you can identify with each flower or scent, and even mixtures of oils perhaps. But start to engage your sense of smell at the food counter, at the supermarket, on the train commuting home from work, in a restaurant at lunch. Try to really notice all the smells permeating the air and let your mind know that you want to be aware.

It's the same with **taste**. Pause when you are eating to really concentrate on the food you eat. One of the exercises we used to do in my seminars was to get people to concentrate on the intensity of each moment of life. I would give attendees one single raisin to eat, and I would make them concentrate on it for a while. You may want to try this yourself.

Action Step: Buy a pack of raisins and put just one in the palm of your hand. Look at it for a few minutes, turn it over. Make a careful note of its shape, its length and size, its color, and notice where the dimples are and so forth. After you have concentrated on your lone raisin for a while, place it in your mouth. But rather than swallowing it right away, move it around, taste it, feel it, chew upon it ever so slowly.

As you chew, imagine the sun shining in someplace where the raisin grew like California. See how the light filtered into the grape and how it made it into your personal sugary, sweet, very special raisin. Go through the eating of the raisin in slow motion. What you discover at the end of this exercise—which by the way we used to call "raisin your consciousness"—is that the raisin becomes the most delicious, most wonderful raisin you have ever tasted. Why? Because you have imbued your concentration upon it. You heightened your sense of it to become aware rather than eating the raisin in the sleep state of mechanical man. You have eaten it as an aware person, aware of the gift of sunshine that's trapped inside the raisin, which of course is the life force.

The sun is an external manifestation of the life force, the God force. So life is more than just feeding your face. You are in this sacred blessing called life, momentarily accepting this little piece of God force that is raisin shaped. Imagine how your relationships and love affairs would be if both of you imbued them with the same intensity as the raisin consciousness exercise.

Concentration is actually a form of love. When you fall in love, you are concentrating on one particular person, and you make them special because you love them. As you concentrate on things, your actions, your life, a raisin, a lover, whatever, you are performing the act of love. By concentrating new love, and by loving, you become more spiritual and more aware. You reconnect to your inner knowing, and the sixth sense.

Just in the act of desiring to see and notice more in taking time to really listen in becoming sensitive to temperature changes and pressure changes, in feeling your sense of touch, in developing your sense of smell and taste, in becoming more central and less dull, you are becoming a more sentient being. It's the act of saying, *I want love in my life. I want to live and know and belong. I want to experience the fullness of my humanity, and wake up to the five senses so that I can activate the sixth and that will take me into an even lovelier world.*

So wake up to the world and step from the egocentric nature of a tick-tock evolution that is poised inside its own minute reality, its own desires, its own neuroses, put that aside and become aware of the energy around you. Ask what's happening here, at a subtle level, what smells, what tastes, what sounds and feelings. What is the subtle overall energy message here? Instantly, the universe responds. It talks to you and tells you things. It doesn't take years of practice, like golf, it's instant, within a few seconds. If you want to see, it's there. If you want to feel, you will feel. That's how you will make the sixth sense happen.

As you begin to make this journey into sensuality and perception, you travel from the intellectual, logical, scientific world, to a world of sense and sensuality, vision, and phenomena into the sixth sense, which is the doorway to another dimension. You will expect the unexpected; you will see how the process is changing your life. And you will know that logic is fine.

But there is a whole evolution to step to that is not necessarily logical. To comprehend that, you will want to develop a strong inner dialogue with self, not just listening to the ego, the waking conscious, but delving into the subconscious. So bit by bit, you will become aware of the symbols and pictures that exist in your greater memory inside of yourself. Of course, you will want to heighten your subtle energy, the etheric, but that is the key to other-world perception. But it comes once you have reclaimed your sentient self. And once you have entered into the subtlety of the five senses.

When the universe talks about symbols of life, some people don't understand what it is saying. They don't know what the symbols of life mean. For most it is a bit like being plopped down in Czechoslovakia, and I don't speak Czechoslovakian so the symbols are a problem. In the next chapter, I will give you my version of the Czechoslovakia phrase book that explains the symbols of life and the etheric web, your subtle energy.

3

Interpreting the Mystery of Life Symbols

There's a huge difference between thinking of yourself as the center of everything and becoming everything.

To understand life, in its subtle complexity, you have to gradually melt the perceived distance or gap between your mind, both conscious and unconscious, and the outer reality of life that you perceive to be at a distance from you. We train ourselves to close that gap so that all of life becomes an internal external symbol of self.

In other words, things aren't just happening out there; it all has meaning. Once you erase the boundary between the inner you and the external you, what you see and experience is, in effect, an outer representation of that innermost you, and often that inner self is talking to you.

The symbols you see in life reflect who you are, though you may not understand them all at first, as they are rather complex. To melt the barrier and to understand the symbols, it's best to start with learning about these symbols you access via dreams. If a presenter starts to talk about dreams in a presentation, most people fall asleep quite quickly, but bear with me here because being able to correctly analyze your dreams is a first step toward a greater understanding, and it teaches you how to melt the distance between you and the outside world. It also shows you how to understand life symbols and coincidences.

Remembering your dreams is important to your overall development. It teaches you to unravel the language of the subconscious mind. Some of that will come from dreams, but most of the really good stuff comes to you via meditation and visions.

Action Step: Get a notebook and start to write down any dreams you may have during the night. If you think you don't dream much, set your alarm to wake you up several times a night. You'll find the dreams in there or scurrying about in your subconscious mind. Record them. Also in your notebook, write down any visions or sensations that come to you during your dreams or perhaps during meditations.

By trying to remember your dreams, you are telling the inner you that you want to access its world; you want to talk to the subconscious and discover its esoteric symbology. In traveling through the mysterious world of the subconscious mind, you access the super consciousness of the world mind, what Carl Jung called the collective unconscious, and the all knowing. Traveling inward, remembering and analyzing your dreams, you're activating your evolution and saying, *Hey, I want to become conscious of what I am, the total me including the parts I know little about or the parts of self, deep within, that I'm only dimly aware of. I want to know the unknowable, past the five senses and beyond.*

Each of these processes builds with the others: dreams, meditation, symbols, discipline, quiet time, developing the five senses. They all help you develop a two-way dialogue with the subconscious rather than what is often a one-way dialogue with a very demanding ego.

If you have not yet read Jung's book *Man and His Symbols*, do so. Jung had it well nailed down. If you know the book, you might consider rereading it. It'll remind you of the subconscious archetypes and the shadow within and the various components of our psychological makeup, the complexity of the personality, and so forth. You don't have to be an expert, but you do have to have knowledge, and Jung's book is easy to read and understand.

How do we get to a higher communication? First you have to really grip the idea that there is no gap between your inner thoughts and outer reality.

Action Step: From time to time see an image of yourself out in front of you at say a distance of 20 yards. Flip your concentration from your physical body to the distant image of you and back again, and try to flip back and forth with your mind with your concentration as fast as possible. If you find it tiring, stop for a moment, for none of these processes are supposed to trouble you. In seeing your image in this way, you establish the idea of you out there and you in here in the physical body at the same time. It helps you; bit by bit it creates an ever-expanding realization. And as your comprehension grows, you melt the defined boundary—that boundary that is inside your perceptions, the boundary between where the external world ends and where your ego self, your personality, and your subconscious mind begin.

In addition, silencing the ego's chatter with the force of your will by disciplining it will help you a whole bunch, and as you take a more galactic perspective, eventually the boundary between you and the rest of the universe goes away and then you're infinite and you're in a constant dialogue with everything coming at you from other dimensions and from the outside world. In the ego's terminology, it's very important to its security to define itself as separate from others—different from "I'm here, okay and good," and everybody else is over there and less okay.

This is how the unaware handle their shadow side, by displacing the negative and separating themselves from it, along with denying it within themselves.

This works quite well for a while, for within the absence of any other inner voice, the ego can reign supreme. But in the inner world of the spiritual self, you are infinite, and there is no distance between you and everyone else, between you and your subconscious mind or your shadow, or even you and the entire universe. It is all interconnected.

There is a theory that says that when you hold your breath and blank your mind simultaneously, your subtle energy instantly expands to the very reaches of the universe, and twangs back all in the tiniest nanosecond you can ever imagine. I like that theory. I'm constantly holding my breath and clearing my mind and imagining myself traveling to the far reaches of the universe.

The visualization helps me feel complete and everywhere rather than incomplete, fractured, and just here on the physical plane. This process is another version of the same mind flip I talked about a moment ago—

I'm here and over there, and I'm back here. It is the rudimentary beginnings of shape shifting in which the adept can move their consciousness in and out of normal reality and give the impression to others that they are momentarily a bird or an animal or something completely different, or even at some totally different location. It's a shaman's trick.

We think in terms of infinity being out there somewhere, and we look up at the night sky, and we watch the stars and the UFOs going past. And we think, *Wow, there is infinity.* Of course, infinity is an internal as well as an external concept. And so in order to incorporate all of the information available on the physical plane, you have to become bigger than the physical plane. You have to begin to embrace that infinity—meaning, you have to become larger than life in your feelings.

That doesn't mean you become more important than others, more glamorous or more special, just bigger and grateful and humble and silently big. I'm talking about an expansion of self, a self that is already infinite, but expanding. It's much like our universe, which is not expanding into something, but it is expanding, as galaxies move away from each other, creating more space in between themselves. Imagine them as dots on the surface of a balloon. Blow up the balloon and the dots move apart. That's how to imagine an infinity that is expanding.

Your infinite self is expanding in the same way as the universe is as you allow more space for it in your life, as you develop and enhance it. As you move from the confines of the gravitational orbit if you like to have a finite perception and the cramped quarters of an uncomfortable ego, and as you free yourself from the idea of the ego at the center of everything, to the idea of your infinite self that incorporates everything. There's a huge difference between thinking of yourself as the center of everything and becoming everything.

At the beginning of your spiritual journey when you're tick-tocking along as an ordinary person, nothing means anything and you're not in a dialogue with the symbols of your inner self. And neither do external symbols mean anything in particular. However, as you turn inward, then even externals mean something, especially external symbols or events that are strange and unusual.

For example, if you're just looking at a tree, and the leaves are wafting around in the wind, that's nothing in particular. But if suddenly the leaves fall on the ground, and a little creature jumps down from the tree and grabs three of the leaves and runs off, that means something. Suddenly you're watching the universe talking—the leaves and the little critter and the preciseness of the moment and your presence in that moment to observe the event make it an external manifestation of you because you're there to watch it.

The question is what does this event mean? The meaning rests primarily in a degree of endless potential meanings. How many potential meanings there are is not important. What is important is what does the observation mean to you? You are there at the precise moment watching the leaves. It's personal, if you know what I mean, real personal.

What is this event saying in your feelings? You have to delve into the symbol and then put it into the context of your life.

First, let's talk about the delving. Fritz Perls came up with a good method for the delving in his Gestalt therapy work. His method, as a psychotherapist, can explain both external symbols in the waking state and the internal symbols of dreams and reverie. I'll fly through the interpretation system for dreams hopefully without putting you to sleep. So you can then apply it to external symbols as well.

The standard dream interpretation technique developed by Perls goes like this: You have to go back into the dream and analyze each symbol one at a time to see what they mean to you. Usually you can't do that just after you wake from a dream, for the dream takes place at a low level of brain speed, and it comes from the subconscious so you can't properly translate it with the waking brain whose speed will be somewhere between 14 to 22 cycles per second. And you can't necessarily engage the intellect because it doesn't usually know what the subconscious means by a particular symbol.

To understand the dream, therefore, you have to first write it down so that you don't forget it. And then you wait until you have a bit of quiet time. If you can enter into an altered state of consciousness in a meditation, perhaps, you can enter back into the dream from your memory. And because now you're at a quiet state of mind at a slower brain speed because you're meditating or you're relaxing or you're thinking about the dream, you will be able to access your subconscious mind more readily and more effectively.

The famous Perls interpretation was a dream someone recounted they had had of a man walking along with a fishing rod over his shoulder. He walks under a bridge, and then various other things happen in the dream. His method of dream interpretation requires you to act out the dream in your mind's eye, placing yourself first in the man in the dream as he goes along, doing whatever he does.

So you say, I am the man in the dream, and at this point, you put your name in: *I'm the man in Harry's dream. I am the man walking along with a fishing rod, I feel—*, and as you say, *I feel,* you then wait for the character from the dream to tell you how he feels. In other words, what does he symbolize? You go back to the character in your dream. And you ask him what does he symbolize? Or how does he feel?

The man then goes on to say, *I'm going to the river because—,* and as you asked that question, as you give that man in the dream the dialogue, deep from your subconscious mind comes the answer, *—because I want to discover myself, —because I hear the river is full of abundance, and I need abundance in my life,* or whatever the character may answer will teach you things about yourself.

And you wait for that answer. So you're in this sort of interplay with the character, on the one hand, and your intellect on the other. Then you ask the character, *What does the river symbolize? What does he symbolize?* And he will say, *I symbolize or mean—,* and then as he talks to you, he tells you, and the answer comes to you from the subconscious.

Once you've been through the dream, and understood the symbology of the man that's walking along, you then travel in through the other main symbols. In this case, you would now take the part of the fishing rod, and you have to imagine that the fishing rod can speak so you make it come alive. And you have the fishing rod saying, *I am the fishing rod in Harry's dream, I represent—,* and it talks to you, so it responds with whatever it responds. Let's say the fishing rod says, *I represent direct action,* or *I represent the ability to bend to circumstances* or whatever this fishing rod means to you.

Your answers come up from the subconscious. Suddenly as you are analyzing the fishing rod, you remember that, in the dream, the fishing rod whacked the bridge, as the man was walking under, and it bent and you realize that let's say for example, you are perhaps a little too stiff over certain matters in your life and your subconscious is saying, *Hey, bend, Ducky, or you'll whack your head.* So the symbol starts to talk to you. Then you go through each and every symbol of the dream—the bridge, the river, and so on. And each component talks to you and gives you the total story.

Each symbol in the dream and each action is a word in the sentence or in the paragraph that the subconscious is trying to impart to you. Analyzing your dreams is important for it helps you understand the circumstances of your life. It also helps you understand your visions.

Now go back to the little critter that you saw grab the leaves underneath the tree. External symbols like this can represent either some part of your waking intellect, your waking personality, it may describe some recent incidents or psychological aspects of your life. Or the little critter may reflect a part of your deep inner self, the subconscious self—both are possible. Because the critter may reflect a part of your waking external life, a symbol of action you're watching may describe circumstances in your life that you can identify with right now. In that way, you can attempt the interpretation from the intellect right there and then to see if the critter is actually a manifestation of the external reality that you're living.

Ask yourself if the action of the animal and what it does with the leaves is the same as any particular aspect of your life. Look carefully at the overall picture of the action and see if it throws up some kind of congruence, for often the action speaks for itself. Perhaps the critter was picking up the leaves and collecting them, which symbolizes thoughts that you've been having over the last few weeks about how you ought to go collect your debts or you ought to order your life and clean out your basement or whatever it might be.

Sometimes the critter is talking to you from an external view, an external action that you have taken or you've been thinking about taking. If you don't get an immediate clue from your life circumstances, then the symbol of a little critter is reflecting some deep inner part of you. And you'll have to make a note of what the critter did with the leaves. Write it down in your notebook, and later on in a meditation go into the subconscious and slow your brain speed down through meditation and pick out the symbols.

First, the critter, then the leaves, then the trees, one at a time, in the same dream interpretation as Fritz Perls uses going through each one of those symbols and having it talk to you. Bit by bit, you begin to understand the external symbol in relation to your subconscious feelings that are in the subconscious memory. After you've delved into the meaning of the symbol, it's helpful to put the symbol into context of your life.

Sometimes the symbol you see can reflect your immediate consciousness. Ask yourself, *What was I thinking the second before the leaves blew down from the tree and the little animal appeared?* Alternatively, you might ask yourself, *What has been my overall question or problem recently. What is the dominant issue in my mind?* By putting the symbol in context of your current consciousness, you'll find a link there, and you'll see the symbol speaks to you out of current issues. As I said before, it may be talking to you out of your subconscious reality, but either way that symbol as a part of you.

Sometimes external symbols will be ganged together several at a time. So you'll see a man fall off his bike, and later that day, you see a tile come off a roof and a taxi whacks a truck, all three symbols are in the same cosmic sentence. They form a storyline and probably what they're saying is they're talking to you about a special seminar the universe runs sometimes called balance and imbalance, and you'll see perhaps how your life is too helter-skelter, too stressed out, and you'll remember how you bashed your hand against the elevator door that morning. And you'll think to yourself, *Slow down, bro, slow down, sister.* This is what the universe is trying to tell you by your looking at this taxi slamming into a truck.

Watching life symbols is important, and dream recall and analysis is a part of the same process, one inner, the other outer. So write down, remember, and analyze incidents, symbols, and messages coming to you from outside of yourself in daily life. For more often than not, you'll see the same message in your dreams and your visions. As you're now becoming a multi-directional being, there is no outside or inside. There's only infinity in all directions. Sometimes if you can't unravel a symbol right away, and if there are no other symbols close to it that suggest an answer, the symbol will rest in your notebook and it may have to come to you later. Some symbols you see are even predictions or signposts to the future.

One night in a meditation, I saw a vision of two stars in the sky quite close to each other, one lower and one higher. I couldn't figure out what the stars meant to me, so I just jotted it down in my computer file to remember it. Later that year, I was in Australia and I noticed the stars Sirius and Canopus looked exactly like my vision in the way that they were placed in the sky. They caught my attention, and I watched them for a few nights in a row. There were just small lights in and around those stars from time to time flying in strange patterns. I thought them to be satellites, but they'd fly one way and stop and then fly back the other way. Sometimes the little lights in and around Sirius and Canopus flew in formation, and I'd see three of them at a time going one way and another one coming back the other way.

I started flashing that area of the sky with a powerful lamp that has a million candlepower. I continued flashing every clear night for the next several weeks, and eventually the moving lights that I'd been watching between these two stars, to my absolute amazement, flashed back. It was wonderful and eerie at the same time.

Now when I say flash back, I'm not talking like twinkle twinkle little star, I'm talking enormous flashes like if you held your thumb up in the sky, the flash would be as big as your thumbnail and enormously bright, and the flashes followed a mathematical sequence so they weren't random. A group of my friends saw this as well. Sometimes the little lights flashed while moving in slow motion, and other times they flashed their lights while moving into extremes of velocity traversing 60 degrees of sky in seconds.

All this flashing back and forth to these characters up there at Sirius and Canopus hasn't changed my life or anything like that. For the rent is still due and the trash has to be hauled, but it's a bit of fun and it's taught me things. The experience helped me to reaffirm that galactic-ness, that sense of, yes, I'm a human here on the Earth plane. But there's a whole bunch of stuff going on out there that we don't know about. And you never know the flashing lights may evolve into something.

Often symbols progress over the years and things develop from them.

If a symbol comes to you, as a result of that you make a small adjustment in your life for the better. It's very much like an aircraft that makes, let's say, a 1 degree turn in flight. One degree makes a huge difference to the aircraft's eventual destination. In life, it's the same small adjustment today that doesn't seem that important, but if you look back at that 1 degree turn that you made in your feeling, say ten years ago, you'll see how that slight change carried you to an entirely different place, and a completely different way of looking at life.

Begin to Claim Your Power

At this point in your journey, you have to step up and begin to claim your power. By that I mean that you have to demand that each of your faculties—your mind, your feelings, your emotions, your metaphysical energy, your intuition, and your extrasensory perception—begin to exercise their prowess, their perception. In other words, as a part of developing the sixth sense, you have to demand that it be there for you.

Now that you have a better grip of symbols, let us get the sixth sense going and exercise it and pull information from our surroundings.

Action Step: Start with this: prior to telephoning somebody, visualize their home, see if you can pick them up in your feelings, see whether or not your feelings tell you if they're there. The trick is to see a friend as a feeling, not as a physical person.

In other words, what is the overall feeling of the person you're looking for? We remember people by the feeling that their character and overall energy give off, not by the shape of their face. Think back to someone you knew at school, or someone you haven't seen for years. You won't be able to remember their face in much detail, if you can remember it at all, but you can remember their character and the feeling that came from their character and personality.

When looking to contact a friend at a location, look for the feeling that you're familiar with and see if the feeling is at the location where you want to call. Can you feel if they're at home or not? See how often you're right. Don't worry if you get it wrong by asking a lot. Your batting average will improve quickly. [This material was written well before cell phones changed our calling habits.]

The important point is that you start asking questions of your inner power. Establish a non-logical link to higher perception and inner knowing. With it, you can look around corners or into the future; you can perceive what is logically imperceptible. But you have to begin to convince yourself if you're not already convinced from previous experiences that you have the power. It's mostly a matter of developing sophistication and expertise rather than hit or miss. Expect to be right 100 percent of the time.

Action Step: When a person is talking to you, try to reach out and touch them with your feelings. This is like visualizing yourself with a long arm and pulling back toward you a molecule of that person's heart, a molecule of their overall feeling for you to perceive and comprehend and understand. That's not to lessen their energy in any way; you're just taking a small sample. Reach into their heart where the heart chakra spins in the center of the chest and imagine yourself grabbing a subatomic etheric sample of them. In this way, you're pulling a molecule of the feeling back toward you.

Now mentally ask how this sample feels. It will tell you much about the person's overall emotion, just as the symbols in your dreams will tell you about what they represent. And the person that you're sampling may be very different from their words or their current demeanor. As you reach out and you pull a bit of them back toward you, you learn about how they actually feel, not how they say they feel.

When you're in conversation with others, ask yourself how well what this person is saying sits with you. In other words, what is the subtlety of the communication here? Is it truthful or not, scattered or solid, reasonable or flaky? By asking these questions, you begin to say to yourself, *Hey, wake up, I want to know where this person's at. I want to know what these people around me are feeling.*

This may feel a bit strange testing out your powers before you've had a chance to develop them. But it is partly through the testing that you create your development. In other words, there's no proper development of the power until you start acknowledging it and using it.

As long as your approach is not scattered or haphazard, if you access the power in a disciplined and powerful way, all will be revealed. The exercises and concepts presented here and in the other chapters will help you because, as you've probably noticed, they are designed to spread you out to make you bigger and to connect you to the power. They all help, but it's only through practice and intention that you carry the concept of the sixth sense into day-to-day reality. The important thing to remember is that everything inner and outer emits a feeling, and that feeling has an identity—a thumbprint of energy.

A building, for example, even though it is inanimate, has a feeling because emotion and energy were put into the building when it was built. People have feelings about the building—they like it, they don't like it, they work there, they don't work there. It's functional, it's valuable, they earn money from it or whatever. The building takes on a personality or character through the energy with which it is imbued.

So as you walk along now and observe, each and every day, twenty or thirty times or more, if possible, as many times as you can possibly manage, ask yourself, *How does this thing in front of me right here feel?* Push out your feelings into people and things and situations. The process is nothing more than grabbing a bit of energy, as I described, or you can just exercise your attention upon the thing or persons in question and suck back to your heart a bit of the energy, a quantum mechanical unit, like a vacuum cleaner.

Another way to perform this energy collection process is to see yourself with a ray of light going out from you. Imagine the ray with a hook on it. It goes out, grabs things, and brings a little bit back to you to examine. If you are in the street, start to pull from inanimate and animate objects. How does an animal feel? The birds, how do they feel? Pull from the inner character of the bird and ask yourself the question, how does it feel? Do you feel that specialness in the bird? How do the buildings in the shopping mall feel? Grab samples of the people there. There's a nun on a skateboard hurtling through the park. How does she feel? There's a homeless person with a teddy bear sleeping next to copies of the financial pages of the *Herald Tribune*? How does that feel?

Practice with lots of people and situations and things and get used to this process. Especially do it every time you meet someone new that you know little or nothing about. You'll be amazed how quickly you'll be able to read inside people.

Action Step: The way to become proficient is to practice on hundreds and hundreds of people. Sit on a bench at the shopping mall. Do one person after the next. Try not to be influenced too much by the way people look. Sometimes the way a person looks is an external manifestation of how they feel; however, very often it isn't, so you want to go past the visual information they emit and just pull from their energy. Don't look at the person in too much detail. Perhaps you might try keeping your gaze down so that you don't see the top half of their torso as they pass. Even looking down, you can still mentally reach out and pull a molecule of them back toward you.

As you do, you'll come into a sense of how they feel, you'll know things others don't. As you enter the world of sensuality, sensitivity, and feeling, you instantly become bigger in your energy. The universe responds by training you and showing you things you don't already know.

Then you can ask your friend if he was at the bowling club yesterday at three o'clock because you saw him in your feelings. If he says no, don't worry about it, it doesn't matter if you're wrong ten times out of ten at the beginning anyway. You have to go past that very human tendency of not wanting to feel like a complete idiot. Making yourself vulnerable is part of the process of committing to your subtle impressions and making them important—even if many are wrong at the start. When you're not committed, your inner self doesn't take you seriously. It's almost as if it can't be bothered to get things right as it knows you don't care. It knows you will override its voice or feelings with the intellect.

This level of need and desire for information is important. If the rest of your life depended on the very next extrasensory perception being right, then the inner you will make sure it gets it right. It's strange, but that's how the system works. Going past the discomfort of being wrong is part of how you train yourself to be right.

When you get a perception, providing it is reasonable, and it hasn't told you to jump off a cliff because it thinks you can fly or something weird like that, try to act upon that impression. In other words, if you feel your friend is at the bowling club, and you want to see them, drive over and check it out. Taking action as a result of your inner perceptions is another way of affirming its validity.

Sometimes those actions will lead you down a dead end. Or it'll take you over to the bowling club for no reason at all, but that's part of the process. So don't worry about it. Just come out of the bowling club, turn around, and leave.

When I trained to be a spiritualist medium in London at the College of Psychic Studies, one of the main techniques they taught was that communicating with the spirits really isn't that difficult. It's just a matter of opening the chakras and pulling energy up through the chakras to the crown. The spiritualist training involved mostly going past the inhibition of making a complete idiot of yourself.

During the training, we would sit in a circle and open the chakras. I'll discuss more about that in the next chapter. And we would bring energy into our circle and speak our truth, whatever we saw in the mind's eye, no matter how fleeting the impression. It didn't matter if we were wrong. The process was one of going past the inhibition of being wrong.

The trick for you is the same. Ask, ask, ask every day until you get to the point where you more or less are perpetually right. Talking to dead spirits is not most people's cup of tea, and it isn't mine anymore either. It was just a part of my training, but everything helps you learn. Perception can be turned in a million directions that will empower and enhance you. To really embrace your subtle energy, you'll have to start to meditate each day if you don't already do so. Even just a few minutes each day, but your meditation should be regular and at the same time.

The practice is an important part of opening you up. It helps you control your mind so you can exercise more domination of your life. Meditation also helps you expand the etheric energy around you. It establishes a serenity from which the feeling base of your power grows.

There's a stage in everyone's spiritual journey where they have to allow themselves to become vulnerable if they want to experience more energy, more power. To win everything, you have to loosen your grip somewhat. Let go of your grip on fear, self-consciousness, and inhibition so you can travel on from here to somewhere different and better. It's a matter of trusting and going with the flow and knowing that you don't have to know all of the time. It's a fact of your spiritual journey and your ever-increasing energy that you won't know so far in advance what you're doing next, and you'll be more spontaneous and will have fewer rules and regulations in your life, less restriction.

Your whole approach to life becomes less rigid—you're open to offers, so to speak—and you're ready to hop the great freight train of life because you're going places. I need to give you some special etheric exercises at this point to kick-start you along. Also I want to talk about the importance of imagination. In the next chapter, I'll show you a couple of subtle ideas that will help you develop the expanse of your mind. It's part of the opening.

4

Hidden Secrets
of the Etheric

The etheric is the subtle emanation that exudes from your body. In certain circumstances, it's visible to the naked eye. It's easy to learn to feel it. For years, scientists have said that the etheric is not there. But now they are coming around to the idea that it might be there, but they don't know what it really means. And they don't give it much influence or credence yet, but I predict in time it will become the single biggest breakthrough in perception, medicine, and science that has ever been.

Acupuncture, which stimulates the flow of chi along the meridians, is the rudimentary beginnings of etheric healing. Imagine the sages who discovered acupuncture knew more than modern practitioners, and that the secret of the etheric was lost somewhere in our ancient history. The sages who knew the etheric technology would heal by lying beside their patient and rolling their etheric out of their own body. In this way, they would enter into the patient's body, with their etheric energy, and once in there, they could perform even minor operations and energy adjustments, and they could create a movement of energy within the patient's body for the patient's benefit.

Once we understand the etheric, we can command the energy that is at the root of our health and well-being.

I have had a few discussions with some of the modern alternative healers, and we have talked about how this type of healing was done. Yet in this area of healing, we are still all stumbling along, but through trial and error, we will get it ultimately, or our children will or their children will, but it will come. The etheric is the next step.

Healing is not my expertise, but I have worked on the etheric for over twelve years, especially in relation to consciousness. So I know how it moves, and I have also uncovered some of the methodology as to how it links us into other dimensions. I am aware of the flow of the etheric around the body. I have also figured out, in a rudimentary way, how to move the etheric and use it. I would enter trance and could attempt to feel the energy within me. And then I'd come up with an idea of how to move the etheric around.

Some of the techniques I tried were way out. Traveling into the unknown can be a bit weird at times. But I like the challenge of it all, and the sense of adventure, and not many others were doing this sort of stuff. There are no books on it. I blogged away on my own for twelve years.

I tried out etheric maneuvers, testing them over and over until I knew that they were foolproof and safe and, most importantly, that they worked. Some of the simplest techniques I tried out with my seminar participants with their permission, of course, and that way I'd know if my techniques worked in groups or not. I was looking for a way of showing people the reality of other dimensions and the reality of the subtle body and the power that's contained there.

Often the participants had little or no previous training, so most of the techniques worked well, which was lovely. Some techniques needed adjustment, and some flopped completely. So I bagged the duds, kept the good stuff, and homed in on improving the others. In this way, I have unraveled over time some of the ancient knowledge, but the greater part of it still remains a mystery.

The etheric contains information about your characteristics, both emotional and mental, and it shows your stock of light, so to speak, your metaphysical reality as well as showing aspects of your physical condition and so forth.

The Chakras

The chakras are vortices of energy that spin through the subtle body. The root chakra is at the base of the spine. The other lower chakras I don't bother with. I have concentrated instead on the four chakras that are easy to feel that I know a lot about, and these are the root, the heart, the throat, and the crown, which is over the top of your head.

I want you to practice this chakra exercise each day if possible. Don't do it right now. Just learn the technique. Once you have got it down pat, it's not hard. You will use it to open up your energy, and you will find that sixth-sense perceptions will flow like the Mississippi River just after the snow melt.

My chakra opening process is a bit different to others that you might have heard of before. In my research, I discovered that some of the teachers who were laying down the basis of modern metaphysical knowledge (like the teachers and writers that taught at the end of the Victorian era and early into the 1900s) made simple mistakes. They got some techniques back to front like the standard chakra opening exercise.

Other techniques that they taught were just flat out wrong. Therefore, I finally made the right adjustments and overrode some of the old information and developed my method. It's not just a nice theory. I have tested it over and over and on myself as well.

Action Step: Find a regular spot to do your meditations, a comfortable place where you won't be disturbed. Lie down if you want, but you are more likely to fall asleep if you are not a real meditation expert. So if you are a bit of a beginner, sit in a chair, get a small concave mirror, one that is bent inward, like a shaving mirror, and place that close to your head. If you are lying down, it should be about eighteen inches from your right temple. If you are sitting, place the mirror to your right on a nearby table or shelf or window ledge where the mirror acts like a satellite dish.

Next, close your eyes. Breathe in and out and relax. Begin by feeling the presence of the mirror near you; bounce your consciousness back and forth off it a couple of times. Now before you get going and before you open yourself up, say to yourself, *I am shielded from any influence that is not of the life force. I invite assistance and cooperation and guidance only from entities or energies whose wisdom and experience is greater than my own. Nothing negative or dangerous can approach me in this experience. So be it. I am light.*

Now move your concentration to the base of your spine, to the root chakra, and visualize energy light going up and down through the center of your body from the root to the top of your head. Do this several times, then rest. This clears a path for the energy to rise.

Next, go back to the root and mentally collect a little bubble of light, say golf-ball size, and bring it up through the center of your being all the way up to the underside of the top of your head. Visualize that light hitting the underside of your skull like *dongggg*. Then allow the bubble to float slowly back down to the root. Do that three times. As you move it up faster each time, try to get the last one to really *dongggg* the underside of the top of your skull at speed. You may even feel it the first time you tried and you will think, *Wow, that's my energy. Cool.*

Now center your concentration back at the root and get another bubble of light and move it up through the center of your being once more. Do it slowly. Come up the inside of your body with the light passing your navel and up through your chest and pause at the area of your heart. Imagine yourself inside the center of your body, mentally visualize the heart chakra opening. So push out from the inside of you and see the spinning chakra unfolding.

This is where my technique is different from the way that the old techniques were taught because they always show you opening the chakras from the outside. In my exercises you are inside the body opening the chakra outward.

Imagine the chakra at the heart as a flower and fold it open like you are opening the petals of a flower—push from within outward and fold it open. Once it's open, move through the chakra with your concentration through the heart chakra to the outside world. Imagine you have a pair of eyes on the little golf ball of light that's hovering at your heart. And imagine you are looking out through the chakra into physical reality into the room around you or at the location where you are meditating.

Then bring the light up a little further through your body to the base of your throat where your neck joins your torso. That is where the chakra is. Open that chakra and, again, visualize yourself pushing out to open it and visualize that little golf ball like it's got eyes and is looking out through your throat.

Then take the bubble of light up to the third eye just above the top of your nose and open that. Push out through the center of your forehead and look through it with your golf-ball eyes once more.

The heart chakra is big compared to the throat, and the throat is much larger than the third eye.

Next, move your concentration to the underside of the top of your skull. So here you have to visualize that you have come up through your brain and you are just underneath the top of your head, inside your skull on the underside. And once you visualize that, imagine yourself punching up through the top of your head, pushing with the force of your will to get the little bubble out through the top of your head.

Now you have your chakras open. How open they are will depend on how vulnerable you have allowed yourself to be in this lifetime. Breathe in and out slowly for a moment and then take a breath and hold it for a few seconds. Keep your mind blank. Visualize yourself expanding to the outer reaches of the universe and back again, as you exhale. You are momentarily poised in an infinite moment in time.

Say to yourself, *I am everywhere. I am in a knowing.* Do the expansion breathing in and out to the infinite reaches of the universe three times. By the way, the expansion breathing doesn't necessarily have to be done in a structured meditation. You can do it anywhere: sitting on a bus, waiting in your car, for example. It's good to expand yourself from time to time, and during the day, it reminds you that you are everything and everywhere. You are part of the light.

As you breathe in and visualize yourself expanding in every direction, be particularly careful to visualize yourself as a multidirectional being, remembering to think what is above you and what is through the ground below you. As humans, we are very aligned to what is in front of us, but we don't think in terms of 360 degrees.

Think of this from time to time. There are stars and galaxies under your feet. Of course, below us is the planet Earth, beyond are other stars, millions of them. In fact, there are as many stars below your feet through the Earth, as there are stars above your head. At the center of the Earth's core is an enormous crystal of iron about the size of the moon. The iron crystal revolves and rotates, and as it does, it creates the Earth's magnetic field. It's a power station radiating energy back up through the ground. You are going to learn to use it.

Scientists have recently discovered that the core is detached from the Earth's crust and that it spins independently from the outer layers of the Earth and slightly faster. So the crystal at the core of the Earth is like a planet within a planet. Through the magnetic field of the core, you can add velocity to your life and to your perception.

So breathe in and imagine the iron crystal in the center of the Earth and hold your breath and mentally bounce a thought off the core—*pinggg*—and expand yourself as the thought ricochets up instantly in every direction, up through the planet Earth to any part of the world on the surface, or to any person or situation at ground level. Or you can ricochet up through the crust and beyond the planet to the outer reaches of the universe, which of course is below you, above you, in front and behind in every direction.

In this way, what you are saying is, *I am beyond time. I operate at infinite velocity, and I am standing larger than life.* There is a crystal mirror inside the Earth, and there is the mirror by your head, and your external life and inner world of dreams and visions are now becoming two mirrors reflecting reality back to you. And these two mirrors—the crystal core of the Earth and the mirror that is by your head in the meditation—both reflect light, they reflect energy, and they create an infinite knock of light that bounces back and forth at high velocity through three dimensions of spatial reality and one of time.

The knock of the light traveling between the Earth's core and the little mirror by your head accelerates energy inside you. The two reflections of light are bouncing back and forth, establishing velocity, and they combine to form a perception, a projection of energy, the power, and the acceleration leads you gently into perception of the fifth dimension. That fifth dimensional spirit world is opposite us mirrored in its relation to us.

I could also say that it seems to be facing us, although there are circumstances when it is not. But mainly it is facing us. It's like looking at another world in the bathroom mirror—that spirit world opposite to you would be facing, you would it not, and it is also reversed left or right.

I know there is a version of time called imaginary time that is mathematically at a 90-degree angle to regular time. And I believe that is correct because I have seen other spirit worlds that are at the same strange 90-degree angle. I mention it all in passing as it was fascinating to me when I first discovered the positioning of these strange worlds. However, the exact position of these other spiritual dimensions may shift all of the time. So what really matters in a practical sense is that the mirror that is by you and the Earth core, the energy transferring between them helps to carry your perception beyond the 3-D world of human perception and into the spiritual worlds where there is heaps and heaps of information that's handy to evolve in humans.

You are learning to use the mirror on the Earth's core in a strange and unusual way to penetrate deep into yourself and into other worlds of inner knowing.

From time to time in your chakra opening meditation, you will bounce your mind off the little mirror to your right down to the core of the Earth and back again and then bounce your mind off the little mirror back and forth several times. Then turn your mind to a distant galaxy, one that is underneath you, for example, remembering that there are as many stars underneath you as above you, and you fire a thought down through the Earth and bounce it off the distant galaxy and feel the angle below you to the distant stars. Notice how that bounce feels different to the thought that you bounced off the Earth's core. You will feel the difference in the angle.

Things are moving along nicely, and now you are ready. You have two satellites, and two other mirror worlds internal and external that you have been working on through the symbology I spoke about in an earlier chapter. You have four chakras open, and you are relaxed, so now you can cast your perception in any direction you wish and work with the spiritual light within you for your greater knowing for your highest good and for the good of others.

Here are two visualizations I want you to perform from time to time, either in the chakra meditation or whenever you have a moment.

Action Step: The first one involves seeing the Earth very small. Stop whatever you are doing and breathe in deeply and visualize the planet Earth in the palm of your hand. See it resting there, very, very tiny. See the situations in life that bother you. See them placed on that tiny planet, and see all of our humanity and all of this planet resting in the palm of your hand. In this way, seeing the Earth literally in your hand, you are saying, *I am bigger than life. Eternal. I control my evolution. I control my destiny.*

This isn't some egocentric, godlike thing where you are setting yourself up as leader of all the people or proclaiming yourself to be better than everybody else. It's just a way of saying you are bigger than the mundane circumstances of this evolution. You have affirmed this silently without making a big deal of it to others. It's your personal affirmation. If anyone is giving you trouble, see them in the palm of your hand as a minute person standing on the little planet and send them love.

Sometimes it's hard to project love to people you don't care for, but do it anyway. Send love and then bring your hand up to your mouth and breathe in and then blow a concentrated puff of air into the palm of your hand at the image of that person who is giving you trouble and dismiss them. Send them away. Allow them to seek an evolution elsewhere beyond your life. Help them to discover that evolution. And don't do it with rancor and hatred. Send them off with hot air and love, which is much nicer and more effective in the end.

Hating people holds them close to you. And often your anger and antagonism rob you of life force. The loathsome feelings can make you sick and stymie your growth and lock you into a nasty situation that you will possibly carry to the grave. That's not a clever idea, believe me.

Action Step: The second of the two visualizations involves seeing yourself straddling the planet. Now the planet is its normal size, and you are above it as an enormous being. You are a colossus standing thousands of miles high astride the Earth, one foot at the North Pole and the other at the South Pole with the equator below you, passing between your feet. In this way you affirm your domination of this existence of yours. You are the powerfully omnipotent, a universal, a part of all things as you put a new perspective, a new dimension into your life.

Finally one last item in this visualization category. The Earth, I believe, has a kind of spirit of its own Gaia. It is aware of itself. It is not an inanimate object. Our Earth has an evolution and knows about its own evolution as you are discovering information about yours. The spirit of the Earth is wise and makes adjustments. It knows things. Talk to the spirit of Mother Earth at times and get into a sacred relationship with that spirit to help you align to the nature self within you. You will be amazed how the Earth will show you things about itself—things that are very informative and most endearing.

Further Chakra Opening Techniques to View the Etheric

The chakra opening process should last twenty-four minutes. After the initial chakra opening exercise, relax, and breathe normally and then see energy coming from the God force through your heart. Feel it coming from within and flowing outward and see it coming from without and flowing inward.

As that energy flows through your heart, engage your concentration upon it and pull the energy up from the heart to the forehead and the third eye chakra. In this way you will activate the third eye chakra and increase your ability to experience visions.

Action Step: If you are in a circle of friends who meditate together, try this. After you have all closed your eyes and opened your chakras, visualize the person sitting to your left and breathe in, and as you breathe out, project your breath to them as light and send them energy. Each circle member does that three times to the person next to them. Then you will move on around to the next person always going around to your left in a clockwise direction.

In breathing each other in and out, you build energy among yourselves. Once that energy is established, a reservoir of energy develops in the center of the circle, and you then mentally pull from that pool of energy up through your heart chakra and you direct that group energy upward toward the third eye. Once there is enough energy light at the third eye, pictures and impressions will appear.

You can talk to each other about what it is you all see as you go along, or you can just remain silent and perceive what you perceive. But whatever you do see, remember it and jot it down later in your notebook so you can ponder it at another time. It is important to keep an ongoing record of impacting dreams and visions, perceptions, and things that come to you. It is part of your affirmation, part of you that saying that the world of subtle reality is important to you.

Gradually, a larger picture begins to develop, and you will see aspects of your life that you don't see now. They may be cloudy or come in little packets, and those packets of perception make up the whole picture.

After the chakras are open, and you have done the visualizations I suggested, take time to pull energy up from your heart chakra to the third eye and the crown and stay still and blank your mind and watch. The inner screen of your mind's eye may be dark for a while, but you have to be patient, and you have to push through that darkness slowly over time. It takes tenacity to get from here to over there.

Meanwhile, you can direct light to any areas of your body that you feel need attention. And as suggested, from time to time, think of the mirror beside you and bounce your mind back and forth off it and bounce off the Earth's core and the distant galaxies and so on and wait and notice what you see.

When the meditation period is over, take a moment to visualize the chakras closed. Do that carefully, one at a time. You don't have to close the crown as it never shuts, just close the third eye, the throat, and the heart. If you worry about being too open, then don't go out into public places for about twenty to thirty minutes after the meditation.

In opening up, one does become vulnerable, so when doing this meditation exercise, you should avoid mind-altering drugs, alcohol, and negative people or locations imbued with negative energy. It helps to avoid burial grounds and cemeteries.

I was meditating once at the Great Pyramid of Giza. I had been inside the king's chamber for several hours at night when the place was officially shut. That was fine, but later in the morning I walked outside and meditated at the foot of the pyramid. I discovered more earthbound spirits around that thing than there were tourists climbing over it. I shoved off to breakfast double quick. Don't get unduly hung up about negative influences or energies taking you over. It can't really happen unless your energy is incredibly low or you are into the dark side.

As long as your energy is normal, and you're not into weird stuff, heavy drugs, black magic, or sadomasochism, you will be fine, trust me. By the way, if during meditation you ever come upon a negative energy from the astral world, don't be scared of it because it can't really harm you. Pull up your strength, look it in the eye, and tell it to bug off. As you do so, expel a breath of air, directing it in your mind's eye toward the entity or energy that you are dealing with.

It's amazing how well this technique works. Negative energies rely on your fear and weakness for their validity. Any decent show of strength and they melt away in horror.

Explore Your Finite Being

Just as I was talking about imagining the stars below you, here are a few more mental exercises to try in relation to your being a multidirectional infinite being—a person with a large vision, not a small one. It's important to concentrate on what is above or below and behind you, as everything that is in front of you more or less takes care of itself. The process here expands your etheric energy, enhancing your overall mindset, and places you geographically in an infinite galactic mind-set everywhere at once.

Normally, one faces forward unless, of course, you turn your head, but your subtle energy can be directed via your will and imagination in any direction you wish. You should think in terms of turning it around from time to time and moving it in unusual directions. It doesn't matter if you perceive it happening right away or not. It is in the thinking about it and trying it that you get going and in moving your subtle energy, you establish a higher velocity, for normally the etheric in most people is quite sluggish and moves only in response to a motion. It's very exciting for the etheric when you start moving it around. It responds quickly and becomes most lively. So you will find you have more energy and also that you need less sleep.

These directional exercises I am about to go through can be performed almost anywhere, as you trod along through daily life.

Action Step: Let's say you are at the supermarket waiting in line at the checkout. Mentally visualize yourself turning around. Don't move your body, but etherically imagine yourself turning and walking out through the back of yourself. Then see if you can etherically reach out and touch the person behind you. As you touch them, see if you can get the etheric to give you information about that person, even though you haven't turned around to look at them.

Once you have the information, ponder it for a second and then turn around and see if the information you got was correct. By the way, you visualize your etheric as a blue-gray mist. It is you-shaped—meaning it is shaped the same as the physical you, and you have to know that you can mentally direct it with your will in whatever direction you wish.

Action Step: Let's say there's a person in front of you in the line at the checkout. Collect your thoughts, blank your mind, and mentally put out an etheric hand and tickle the back of their neck. See if you can get them to turn their head. If they don't move right away, imagine yourself up really close to them, lick the back of their neck, make the visualization big as if you have a very large tongue and you are giving the person a wet, sloppy cow lick right at the base of their neck. If they are not too distracted by their own thoughts, they will feel it and they will turn around.

You see, what I am saying here is that you are not confined to the geographical position of your body. You can move your subtle body without moving your physical body. Of course, right now, you would have to rely on feelings inside that subtle body to perceive things. But eventually you will be able to see through the etheric body, and then you realize that you are not limited in vision to where your physical eyes are. You will be able to move your eyes around, so to speak, from one side of the room to the next and from one part of the planet to another.

This technique is very handy for looking around corners in life. As humans we define reality as a small band of deception that is slightly less than 100 degrees wide. That line of direct sight is in front of us; everything else is blotted out or made less relevant. For the most part, we ignore our peripheral perception, yet we would need if we were to become a multidirectional antenna picking up energy from every direction. Your peripheral perception is much more sensitive than your regular sight. You have to engage it if you ever want to see the etheric.

So from time to time, start concentrating on your peripheral vision and ask yourself what is to your left and what is to your right. Don't move your eyes. Keep them straight ahead and just move your concentration to one side of your peripheral vision and then to the other.

Action Step: To help you practice, get a pair of old glasses, sunglasses are fine, and tape the lenses over with tape that you can't see through. Put the glasses on and walk about the house carefully for half an hour or so. With your forward vision impaired, you will become more aware of your side vision. Try not to move your eyes too much, just let them stare through the center of the glasses at the tape that you have pasted onto the lenses. Do this from time to time as part of your affirmation to reactivate your peripheral perception.

Etheric is a word that comes from the Greek word *ether*, which means to blaze. In the metaphysical sense, it is the subtle subliminal energy that your mind and body give off. In the olden days, it was believed that ether was an invisible substance that filled the universe. It was later proved, using calculations of the motions of the Earth through space, there is no ether out there. The proof of the nonexistence of ether relied on the motion of the planets.

But now a new hypothesis has come out of the superstring and GUT, the grand unified theory, that now suggests that there might be an ether, which perhaps we would be able to detect if the planet were not moving through the cosmos as it does at about 30 kilometers per second. I call this subtle body the etheric because that's what it was always called in bygone days.

The word was chosen by the Victorian writers and researchers and used widely in the writings of the Theosophists, who are those who teach about God based on mystical insight. They visited India in the late 1800s, early 1900s. Whether or not the word is appropriate, because we don't know if there is an ether in the cosmos (and it doesn't really matter, as it doesn't affect the reality of your subtle body).

The etheric, the subtle energy your mind body gives off, is very different from possible subatomic particles that may or may not be swishing around in the heavens. I think that's important to clarify that point. Of course, the energy of your etheric must be made up of subatomic particles, but when the energy is expressed around the body, it is definitely not in its subatomic state. For if it were, our vision would not be able to see it.

Think of it like this. We can't see a water molecule, but we can see the effect of trillions of water molecules when they are grouped together in a cloud. The etheric is the same way. So I don't know what you are looking at when you see the etheric around the physical body, whether that is ether in the scientific term. But what I am saying is that whatever we are looking at is an electromagnetic energy of some kind, because it has within it photons of light. And when that light is grouped together, it becomes cloudy looking, and thus visible to the naked eye in certain circumstances.

Also, the sight of the etheric seems to depend upon one's sensitivity and development. It was originally taught by the Theosophists that sight of the aura, as they sometimes called it, was linked to one's spirituality. A high adept would have the sight and a lowly student would not. I believe 95 percent of this idea is wrong, but there is a fragment of truth in it if one looks at the idea from a certain angle, for the adept would have a controlled and disciplined energy, and so he or she would have a greater perception. But that perception does not flow as a reward for holiness. It's just the nature of the etheric energy, because you have to view a person's etheric through your own etheric, and naturally if your own etheric is quiet and serene, your perception is more acute.

In my view, the spiritual elitism of the old writers was a bunch of hooey, and almost everyone can feel their etheric energy with a little training. You can soon learn to see it if you will activate and engage your peripheral perception.

5

Claiming Your Higher Power

Imagination is everything.
It is the preview to life's coming attraction.
—*Albert Einstein*

By way of transition to this chapter, let me review where we are. I talked about standing tall, seeing yourself larger than life, visualizing the whole planet Earth in your hand. The function of these visualizations, and the whole idea of your beginning to access the sixth sense is that you need an extrasensory perception as part of your spiritual journey. It's all part of the idea that says you are close to transcending the physical plane. At the same time, you are close to going past conventional knowledge and the limits of a confined mindset.

I remind you, you are not your emotions. You are an eternal being inside a physical body, operating through a mind that may or may not be experiencing what it considers a pleasurable or negative emotion. Once you detach a bit from the emotions of life, you develop a command of your destiny, and the sixth sense and ESP flows, because its subtle energy is not swamped by excessive thinking and loads of emotions and reactions swishing around the etheric to spoil perception.

You are coming to the point where you can command this incarnation, and many take that to mean that they must be rich, famous, or highly successful. Of course, success is great, but it's not necessarily what your sacred journey is about. In the end, you will want to command your life so that you can concentrate on love and the experience of living.

Commanding your destiny is just being in control of that part of this human experience you choose to be in control of. You could spend the rest of your life fishing by a river and still be an initiate in a higher being in a spiritual evolution. We are kidded into thinking that money, glamour, and wealth mean high energy, and everything else is low energy where imbalance, dysfunction, being out of control, hatred, violence, gluttony, greed, and egotistical ideas are considered low energy. Balance, serenity, compassion, and spiritual ideas build high energy. There is no logical boundary to your perception, because there is nothing you can't pull to you in your mind's eye and place it in front of you and look at it.

So you can see how getting in touch with your inner self through consciousness raising, through discipline and visualizing the power within you, through seeing yourself as an eternal being helps you. So hold your breath and see yourself out there expanding at an infinite velocity. See that you are becoming larger than life. Limitlessness is natural. Once you see it and comprehend it, it's a natural outcropping of your perception of self.

The entire universe is inside your heart, inside your charisma, inside your energy. Potentially, there is nothing you can't imagine and so create. Albert Einstein said, "Imagination is everything. It is the preview to life's coming attraction." Imagination is important for it allows you to dream the impossible dream and to materialize it.

Most people's imagination is poorly developed. TV is partly responsible for this. We don't have to imagine Niagara Falls or the plains of the Serengeti. We can watch it in living color. Our couch potato society disempowers our imaginative capacity. Most people are deathly dull, aren't they? Endless conformity, endless chatter, the same stuff over and over, endless macho and violence and crud on TV, making the nation ill. And the broadcast has rich concepts to disempower people making them apathetic and easy to control.

There are some very weird people on this planet whose motivation is money and power. They seek to control and disempower ordinary folk by getting them hooked on debt and drugs and dysfunction, and by desensitizing them, subtly controlling their minds by policing ideas and using disinformation to create a stereotypical conformity that suits the controllers and the big guys in power.

Will you succumb or will you dream the big dream? Will you have the courage to be different and awaken your power to become an infinite being? Keeping that sacrosanct? The spiritual energy within you intact and well looked after? Will you move up in life and develop a greater vision for yourself through good imagination? Most people daydream a lot while yearning for their lottery win or yearning for someone to come and get them. They are awaiting passively, often pathetically, for an oversized dollop of good fortune to fall on their heads from the great goo goo bird in the sky. *Plop . . .* I'm rich. The bird is cool, which creates instant millionaires.

The problem is that its bowel movements are few and far between. Frankly, you are more likely to get hit by lightning. You can ruin your life wasting time waiting for something that might never happen. One day, you'll pass on, and the great goo goo bird will be there leaning up against the pearly gates with a sheepish grin on its face, shrugging his shoulders, shuffling uncomfortably from one foot to the other, mumbling its apologies. And you could be looking back at a dull life. And maybe you will see how you wasted your time and got nothing done, and you will see how you got too suckered into daydreams of a cushy life and glamour and easy street rather than acting to secure such things.

Daydreams are pleasing to the ego. They both suit up, but they don't usually require any discipline or action. The faculty of imagination when used correctly is different. Imagination allows you to see the future, a new future for yourself. But for it to make sense, for it to be real, there has to be a path from today's circumstances where you find yourself right now to whatever the circumstances or vision is of your future.

Daydreaming, in other words, is the brain in neutral, just ruminating doing nothing. *Imagination*, on the other hand, is thinking, visualizing with pictures and is not so passive. Through imagination, you place yourself in the picture and in the feeling of a future circumstance or condition that you want. In daydreaming, you disempower yourself, saying more often than not, *I am hoping for a break. But I don't really believe in myself. I can't really see myself in the vision properly. And by the way, my ego's real lazy, so it won't allow me to take concerted action and do something constructive.*

Daydreaming is easy, it involves no exertion. Do this instead. If you are going for a distant goal, and you want to direct your imagination in that direction, start by feeling yourself present at that future point in time, and act out those circumstances. Allow your imagination to wander through the scenes, being a part of it, and then come back from that future place and focus your inner vision and intellectual concentration on seeing yourself progressing through the steps that it might take to get you from here today to over there tomorrow. Act the steps out in your mind's eye and see yourself moving toward your goal through the intervening steps. You pull goals to you through concentration, while simultaneously moving toward them through concerted action.

As I often say, yearning for things pushes them away from you, or in the emotion of yearning, you affirm that you don't have the thing that you are yearning for. You set up an uncomfortable energy that others often have to climb over. When you really need something and you are emotional about it, people tend to deny you just because you need it. When you are expressing yearning, you are often robbing energy from others, and they resent it deep down. They don't want you satisfying your emotional needs through such tactics. They feel their energy go down as you pull on them when they really want you to attend to their needs, their ideas. It's an energy war, set up by yearning. Don't yearn, act.

In your imagination, envision the goal granted by putting yourself in the picture. See yourself acting out your desires, rather than striving emotionally to achieve them. Don't lean on the goal emotionally, stand straight, and externally move toward the goal. This is important because great opportunities carry a lot of metaphysical energy. They are heavily laden with goodies. So great opportunities don't really travel very far, and that might sound odd. Let me explain.

Special breaks happen on the spot, rarely at a great emotional or physical distance, or commercial distance. In other words, you have to close in on your dream emotionally and physically and shuffle up to it, so to speak. In order for it to happen, you have to be in the flow, in the loop, in the marketplace of life, acting out your greater vision in order for your big break to find you. This is because important people who will open doors for you don't usually scour the streets looking for others who might need a hand up. Important people are in the loop moving in and around their successes, hanging out just with those who are also in the same loop.

Moving close to your dream, practicing perfecting your skills, gathering information, making contact by showing up in the loop gets you close to the target. Meanwhile, you concentrate on what you have to offer, polishing it up and homing in on the idea. People will only want to join you if there's something in it for them. They often only want to if somebody else wants to, and they don't usually commit unless they know they are sure they will get what they want from you.

In other words, they have to know who you are. And they have to understand what you do. They have to see that you are endorsed and made right by others. Because once they see you in the loop, you are in, you're there. You have an identity, a special worth, you are valuable in the marketplace, and you are establishing a track record in whatever creativity or commercial activity you have chosen.

So let's say you are a singer, and you want to have a big record contract with a major company. You have stepped into the idea of singing in bars and clubs maybe, writing songs, hanging out in the studios. You have a good demo, you know your stuff, and you understand what constitutes a commercial record. Now you have a chance.

Theoretically, with a bit of power and the sixth sense helping, your chances of getting a record contract should be simple stuff. How you are going to get there? First, you will engage your imagination, and you will see yourself with the contract performing perhaps for vast crowds. But you will also see yourself moving through the various steps that will place you as close as possible to the goal, not only geographically, but in your feelings—meaning, do you belong to the idea of success? And does that idea or vision really belong to you? Do you really want what you are going for?

Goals that are too distant in your feelings are wishy-washy and vague and ill defined, and so they have little or no metaphysical power. If you want to make a hit record, give me the names of ten of the singers or bands that are in today's current top hits. Then give me the names of every record that made number one in the last eighteen months.

To make it in that business, you have to know what's happening. You have to be in the business, you have to be aware of what's hot, and what's not, who's up and who's finished. If you can't tell me that top hits that have made it recently, you are not giving yourself in the sixth sense much chance for you are out of the game, out of that part of the global mind that circles around rock music.

If you don't know your stuff, you are in the cold. Maybe you are playing your music without realizing it's miles behind the times. Or perhaps it's cool, but no one wants it. Or maybe you play badly and you need practice. Or maybe you can't generate the right emotions in your music.

Remember, you have to speak to an emotion in people for them to buy your stuff. Also, to have a big hit, you often have to put aside what *you* want and get your ego out of the way and cooperate with many other people and accommodate them. And you have to play music that other people want.

Once you have placed yourself geographically close to your vision by getting in the loop, and if you remain close to the vision in your feelings, you believe in yourself and you affirm you believe by acting out your dream, doing sensible and useful things, then and usually only then will opportunities pop up. Once you are in the flow of your greater vision, there will be high energy and people around you, people who are doing what you want to do. Experts, people who are part of the scene. Now and only now are you close enough to really engage the sixth sense to discover your strongest move, especially which particular person or organization will assist you to materialize your vision.

Also, remember, when you are visioning and imagining, start by mulling over what you will give, not what you will receive. I have gotten tens of thousands of proposals over the years from people wanting help and materializing their ideas. I can't remember even half a dozen proposals that ever mentioned giving. They all ask first, and often without even bothering to say *please*. So your vision can't just ask others to give me this and give me that. Life is a trade-off, isn't it? It's either a win-win money trade-off between you and others, or it's an energy trade-off. And you will have to give of your energy, your enthusiasm, your knowledge, your effort up front, or you will have to compromise or shift a bit in order to get your vision off the ground.

I have seen people lose the opportunity of a lifetime because they were scared of success. Sometimes they lost their big chance because they were just too disorganized. And sometimes they lost everything because their ego got in the way and they became dogmatic and demanding and hard to deal with. They couldn't compromise on the universal creative energy, which is fluid and seeks its own balance. So what will you give energy, money, enthusiasm, and innovation? What's in it for others? As you meditate on your vision, try to home in on anything that is lacking. Do you need to polish your vision up a bit? Is knowledge your problem? What's the plan? Does the plan make sense? Okay, you are in the loop.

Let's view the key people in your mind's eye. Think about them intellectually and logically. But then think about them inwardly with your sixth sense with the following exercise.

Action Step: Open your chakras with the method I gave you before and bring the little bubble of light up from the root to your heart. Make sure you are relaxed and your chakras are open, especially the heart. Now put the people that you wish to review in your mind's eye, one at a time. Imagine them in front of you, as if reflected in a mirror. See them, feel them. Watch them right there in front of you. Be aware if any symbols or feelings come up.

Now pick one person in particular and put them up in front of you. Hold that person there with your concentration. Don't let your mind slip away to other things. Now fire the bubble of light that is hovering inside of you in the region of your heart fired at the person you wish to review. You do this by willing the bubble to move in the direction of the other person's heart. You push it with your will, expelling as a soft but short breath at the very moment you fire the bubble at them. It doesn't have to be done with much force. In fact, the more softly you do it, the better it is. You become more sensitive.

Watch what the bubble does. Sometimes it bounces, ricocheting off the person bouncing back to you in a strange way. The trajectory that the bubble takes as it bounces off them will tell you things. Watch, notice, and remember. Write this experience in your notebook. Everything you see at this level of consciousness inside the sixth-sense faculty is most precise and exact. It all means something.

On occasions, the bubble strikes the heart chakra of the person you are looking at and goes straight up from their heart with enormous velocity, up toward their crown chakra at the top of their head. This is very positive. This is a good person, and they would be open to you and helpful and loving. Sometimes the bubble hits the person and wobbles around like it's drunk, or it orbits around them incoherently doing figure eights around their head. It means they are confused and scattered, and their etheric diverts the bubble in a dis-combobulated way. They won't help you much, and, very likely, they will cost you time and money and effort.

Sometimes the bubble you fire hits them and splats out like a soft tomato, which can mean several things. One is that the person in question is needy; they may have grabbed the energy of the bubble you shot at them and absorbed it. Sometimes it means they are angry, so the bubble kind of dies on the spot as it hits them, and you feel nothing. Or you may be vaguely aware of their anger. Sometimes, if they are not interested in you or your ideas, or they don't care, the bubble dissipates and goes nowhere. So if you get a splattered tomato, don't invest much energy in that direction. Not now anyway, wait a bit, and try again in a week or two, and see if the person's energy has changed. See if the bubble does something different next time.

There are hundreds of possible trajectories and more. By firing the bubble into the etheric, you get a readout. Once you have done it for a while, and you have put a lot of people in your mind's eye and you are famil-iar with the process, it will become obvious what each trajectory means. It comes to you if you practice.

The bubble process is a way of reading energy, a bit like sending a satellite to Mars. You have got a connection out there sending you back information. It's a part of the tapping that I talk about in my books where you enter into people's energy, sometimes at a great distance, and you watch them and send them love and notice and appraise. And you become familiar with their needs, and you act accordingly.

Having watched the bubble go to the various people, you will want to review the situation to appraise your opportunities better in the light of inner knowing. Therefore, pull each person up in your mind's eye again, especially the more interesting ones, and see those people one at a time. See them this time closer to you. Feel yourself to be more in touch with their feelings, their identity, and pull them toward you with your concentration. Now momentarily reach out and grasp a little bit of them. That's like etherically pulling a bit from them, like I told you before.

Who are they in their eternal sacred sense? Don't get hung up on their personality, or how they have treated you recently and so forth. Just observe the person unemotionally with no personal criticism or judgment. Put them in your mind's eye.

Here's the even more sophisticated stuff. To get a more accurate feel of their current emotional attitude, you reverse into them for a second or two at the level or at the dimension of the subtle body. Remember, there is no real distance at this level of operation. They are as close to you as you feel them to be. And as they come to you in your mind's eye, you effectively engage the full force of your concentration upon them.

Put a character in your mind's eye and mentally move your own energy, your own etheric, away from your body so that you imagine it well outside of you, as if you are standing outside of yourself facing away to the distance. Then turn your etheric self around, so now it is facing you; you are looking at yourself. Then will your etheric to step back gently and solidly into the character that you are reviewing.

As you enter, blank your mind and hold very still. Instantly an impression or signal comes off that person you are visiting. You perceive their emotions or their feelings, what's going on with them. Sometimes you feel it and sometimes you will actually see it as a symbol or a sign that they give off. And you will comprehend that sign, as many of them are obvious.

Here's an example how that works. I was doing a deal with a fellow. I had just sent him a revised offer by fax. I wanted to know what he thought about it. As I pulled him up in my mind's eye and stepped back inside him, I saw him wince and hold his nose as if he had stepped on a turd, so I knew that the deal might not float in its current form. Anyway, later, I went back again and saw him throw his hands in the air. He is a nice enough kind of bloke but a bit dogmatic. A demanding kind of guy, and he was reacting a bit like a spoiled child and not getting all that he wanted. But I saw in his arm gestures that he would come to the deal in the end after he wrestled with his wounded ego for a bit. I had no doubt his fax would be on my machine later that night. Such is the power of the etheric.

Using this bubble process, you will get an indication of which is the strongest path for you and you stay away from trouble and low energy situations and low energy people. You will learn to engage your sixth sense to look inside people, situations, deals, and organizations. You will figure out what there is to know before you commit.

Most people are fairly weak but fairly honest, except when they are in a corner. Then there is a percentage of people who are downright scumbags. But they don't hide it. When it's obvious, you just have to avoid them. Because they're so obviously dark, you keep out of their way. But the worst sort of the covert ones who act righteously but are, in fact, closet scumbags, if truth be known. They are the ones you need to turn the full force of your perception on as you notice the darkness, and you will do your best not to judge it. If that's the case, whiz off in the opposite direction, even if it means you have to cut your losses and run.

If you are a positive, loving person and if you stay away from shady deals, and so forth, you rarely meet the scumbags because they usually exist in a dimension of their own. But there's a lot of people out there, and some of the dark ones live right next door. Therefore, you have to watch and not take it personally if a scumbag shows up in your life. Through the law of averages, and the law of physics, turds float, so they drift around a lot. One or two will inevitably float past your door. Stay cool, stay distant, establish good boundaries in your psychology, and let people know what you will tolerate and what you won't tolerate.

As a part of these imagination exercises, do this next exercise.

Action Steps: At night, before you go to sleep, review the day backward in time, from the night time to dawn. And instead of just thinking about the day, go back through it in a mental silence, seeing the pictures of the day. Notice the feelings that were associated with those pictures and actions. This process helps you go from just thinking to more seeing and feeling by reviewing the day from your memory. By using your visual and feeling faculty, you activate your imagination, and you practice your power of visioning.

Then again, you can practice your visualization and imagination during the day. Just quiet your mind and imagine yourself moving your etheric around for a bit of visual practice. So let's say you are at the bus stop. Turn around within your subtle energy, like I have described to you, and walk out of your body facing backward. Then see your subtle body leaning say to the right at an angle of 45 degrees and then to the left at an angle of 45 degrees in the opposite direction. And then bring it back in front of you and lower it to the ground very, very slowly and deliberately. Lower it until your etheric nose is inches off the ground.

You do this with your imagination. See the etheric lowering your etheric to the ground and visiting the ant kingdom for a bit. Remind them of the dangers of feet. They forget sometimes.

Take a little mirror with you as you go through the day, the kind that ladies carried around in their purses in the 1930s and 1940s. See your image reflected there and notice it carefully and realize that's what your etheric looks like when it's outside of you, beyond you. Now swivel the mirror quickly back and forth, like you are signaling. Imagine your image flying off the mirror's shiny surface at speed to some distance spot, like the convenience store across the street and see your image buying itself your favorite snack.

Then imagine it coming back just in time for you to eat the snack prior to getting onto the train. And dream of dreams and think about stuff. Let yourself invent strange stories that you can amuse yourself with, stories that have good imagery and see the pictures of the story in your mind's eye and tell the story to yourself.

From time to time, read a bit of poetry and feel out what the poet is saying. What pictures do the words evoke?

Tonight before dinner, draw a portrait of your cat on the back of a dinner plate. And give the cat a spanner [wrench] for a head and flippers for feet. And paint the picture of the cat green and give the cat a couple of strange mouse tattoos, in the painting of course.

After you have eaten, pop to the basement and conjure up a little symphony with two spoons and a rubber band and any old junk that's down there and record it. It doesn't matter how it sounds. And just before you go to bed, take a warm bath and pour loads of water in it and get a bottle of dishwashing liquid and swirl the bathwater around until you have suds to the ceiling. Watch the bubbles flow down the hallway; there's heaps of fun in that.

Get in the bath and play and play and play and cup your hands together real fast and watch as great columns of soap hit the ceiling, dangling off the light precariously, only to pop down on the cat's head a moment later. Get your mate to join as you show them the routine. There is a game in it. Betting your mate which dollop of soap will fall first.

Now you are warm and cozy and in bed and you have gone through the day backward in your mind's eye. You call upon the powers that be to lead you always to your strongest spot and ask them to please teach you things this night that you don't already know. Ask them to help you to get from here in soapsud land, to over there, the Promised Land. And you remind the powers that be of your humble stance in life. Mention the diligent things you have done today to help yourself and others. You will review what you have to offer the world, and you remember that you were kind and gentle today, and that you thought about others as well as yourself.

You mention in passing that scrawny cow, Mrs. Higgins, who has been throwing trash over your fence, even though you have asked her a hundred times not to. And you will mention how you have remembered to project love and caring and understanding to her, even though she drives you nuts, even though, deep down, you would like to wring the scrawny cow's neck.

You'll mention that, and you'll fall asleep in the arms of angels, and they will show you things. In the morning, you will wake up with those thoughts on your mind because you have preprogrammed it that way. You remember to tell yourself before you went to bed that anything important that came to you in the night should be on your mind in the morning as you wake up.

On waking, you jot it down in your notebook and think about it. You will take a moment to think about all the information you have received in the past and review if you actually acted upon it, or whether you ignored most of it. For the more you ignore the power, the more it dries up. You might think it's sensible to act on what you already know as an affirmation that you are powerful and that you are open for even more information. Then you might think you will have a little sit down with a nice cup of tea. You might think to yourself, *I will push ahead on all this spiritual sixth-sense stuff, and I will take action.*

6

Achieving Goals Through Inner Knowing

The God force is the most kick-ass
sixth-sense tool you have ever seen.

In my work and publications, I talk about aligning to whatever creative energy you wish, such as the greatest artists, the greatest musicians, the greatest business or sports people and so on. It's just a matter of concentrating on a particular superstar performer and learning about them and entering into their energy field at a subatomic etheric level, studying them, and watching them on TV, perhaps, if they are alive, or reading about them and emulating them if they are no longer around. But also stepping inside them using the method I introduced with the bubble in the mirror.

It's like putting on an overcoat of the legend's energy imbued with their creative wonderfulness or their ability on the sports field or in the creative arts, in business, or wherever you see yourself a part of that energy. Their success becomes your affirmation. You feel that you are the same energy as they are, limitless, because you know, at an infinite level, you can pull energy from anywhere. Everything is available to you.

Of course, you will always expect the best. You should polish your thinking so that you make sure you always demand of the universe at large a positive outcome to all of your endeavors. If you are asked what your expectations are, you never want to say, "I am not sure. I don't know. I will do the best I can. Let's hope and pray." You always have to have a perpetually ridiculously optimistic outlook, even when situations are at their worst. If you are not normally particularly optimistic, try it as a discipline.

Next time somebody asks you how you think something will pan out, go totally over the top and say, "Marvelous, fantastic, a huge hit, unbelievably well," and so on. Practice expecting the sun, the moon, and the stars—although the universe may give you slightly less than that. It's always best to ask for everything and expect everything. It helps crank up your energy and helps you see yourself in bigger terms.

I have never been much into shocks and scares as I call them. But a recent bull market in equities has attracted me. So I decided to give it a go, knowing very little about the stock market. I started with $120,000 and within about six months, I had made $75,000. And so now my account was worth about $200,000.

A friend that I trust a lot told me about a technology stock. A good bet, he said. So I took a huge plunge and put three-quarters of my money into it. Everything was fine for a few months, then things changed, and a group of bad guys got into the company and ripped it off. The fraud squads were called in, a boardroom war developed among the directors, and the good guys lost the battle to the bad guys. My sure-bet technology stock became worthless overnight.

My broker called to commiserate. I told him the Dow went up and down, like light and dark, just variations of the same energy. He wondered why I wasn't throwing myself off the roof. My broker doesn't understand the finer points of metaphysics.

Now here is the good part: I looked into my feelings, and I was positive and sure the stock market was for me. One day in a meditation I asked of my inner knowing to give me a stock that would double in the near future. I saw the word *Arkon* flash in my mind. I looked up the stock, and it turned out to be a small, obscure Irish mining company. I bought 100,000 Arkon shares at 23 English pence. I knew nothing about the company, but I believed in my inner self.

The next day after I bought the shares, Arkon started going up, and within a few weeks it got to 33 pence. I had made a good profit and so I sold out. I should have kept it for a bit longer. For now it's worth exactly double what I paid for it, yet Arkon helped my spirits after my recent losses.

Meanwhile, I hung in there some weeks later, meditating on the subject. I had a vision. In it I saw a beautiful placid lake covered in morning mist. I just watched it. Suddenly, there was a roar. Something stirred from deep within the waters of the lake and an enormous castle shot up out of the center of the lake with millions of gallons of water pouring off its roof with its battlements covered with seaweed. The castle came up so fast out of the water, I was shocked at the speed of it all. Prior to getting into stocks I had the idea to make some quick money as I wanted to buy a castle in Europe.

So I saw that the vision was saying, *Hang in there, Ducky. When it comes, it will come very quickly.*

I felt the technology loss that I had suffered was just a bit of bad luck. That can happen sometimes. I decided to go with the flow and plug away. Some weeks later, I was given a recommendation on a weird, completely unknown Australian mining stock. I bought it because of the vision, because of the fact that I had seen the castle come out of the lake. I bought it because it felt right to my sixth sense.

The stock only traded at 2 Australian cents. So I wound up with 3 million of them. Nothing happened for a while, but my mate told me to hang in there. And I believed because of the castle vision.

A while later, he called again and said that the same Australian outfit had a sister company, and he advised me to buy that as well. So I borrowed on margin from my broker who is a good guy and bought shares in the sister company at 36 Australian cents. Now I was totally tapped out, a stock operator with no cash, heaps of margin, loads of outrageous optimism, a vision of a castle coming out of a lake, and huge great chunks of Australian desert that I had bought for virtually nothing.

The parent company started ticking up, but not long after, the sister company went ballistic, jumping 10 and 20 cents a day, and then the parent company ticked up some more. In a very, very short space of time, I mean two or three weeks, everything went mega ballistic, and my portfolio went up and up like the Concorde's vertical takeoff.

I went from struggling and a big loan and lots of margin and $150,000 loss on the technology stock to where I got all my money back and some and now thousands ahead. And I am smiling about my sixth sense.

In truth, what I made on the Aussie stocks won't get me a castle, but it will get me a drawbridge and a moat and a few turrets. And that's more than I had before I started. The point is if your dreams don't come to you right away, and if you stuff it up a bit at first through lack of experience, don't worry. Up and down are just two sides of the same energy. Sometimes life tests you to see if you are all hot air or if you really believe in your visions. Are you the warrior, or the worrier? Are you a tiger or a mouse?

Remember, as part of standing tall and developing your money-making ability and creative potential, you have to have the courage to embrace yourself and who you are. You are your own statement in life. You are your own calling card. You have to believe in yourself. Even if the calling card is a bit dog-eared right now, even if your castle is still a long way off, things can come overnight when the energy is right.

Here is another barrier to clear out of the way. More often than not, we limit our creative potential by the fact that we feel that we have to win other people's approval. We feel the need to justify ourselves to fit in, and we feel the need to be accepted. Yes, you might have to adjust to the vagaries of the marketplace, but you don't want to disempower yourself personally by being too shy or too timid or by letting others limit your dream. You are what you are. Look them in the eye and tell them this is who you are; then be flexible, especially when there is money floating about.

I think the biggest culprits in holding you back are more often not family members who, because of their closeness to you, can impact you and have a major influence on you. Often family members have an agenda of their own. They want to keep you where you are, or they don't want you to show them up as being inadequate, or they don't want you heading out and leaving them back at the ranch looking up the back end of a thousand sheep.

Part of developing the spiritual self and developing inner knowing is having the courage to know what it is that you do believe. Certainly, you don't have to have the path laid out for you for the next fifty years. You just have to know that you have the strength to go to the next step and have the courage to follow through and hang in there.

Of course, once you embark on a journey, more often than not, there is no turning back, is there? As your consciousness grows, you become exhilarated by the flow of the God force in your life. With it comes new perceptions and originality. There is no way you are going to go back to the old ways anyway. The problem is that people tend to follow along in their consciousness for a while. And then they come up against the boundary— the boundary of their intellectual knowledge, or what they feel as a social being.

Perhaps they don't feel they are entitled to more. Perhaps they don't feel very adequate because they come from a humble social background. Or perhaps they don't speak the language of success, so they feel inferior. Don't let these hang-ups hold you back. Push up against your comfort zones. It's easy enough to do that. You just have to invent a series of actions or exercises that you will perform that force you to test your comfort zone.

A standard exercise is if you are scared of public speaking, agree to give a lecture. If you are scared of heights, go rock climbing. Your comfort zone is an illusion. It's there because the ego is there, and the ego defines your position. But of course you are not a defined being, you are an infinite being, and your influence and perception are potentially infinite. You can pull information, money, opportunities from all over the planet. You are not limited to just the family ways or the tribal influence, or the group soul of the local tick-tock.

How much of the force do you believe is possible? Most of the people I meet are usually either very meek, or they don't express themselves well, or believe in themselves, or they do believe in themselves, but they only think of themselves. And they don't think of themselves as an infinite caring, sharing being, and an infinite being that is there for people.

Part of the function and part of the search for the Holy Grail within is coming to a point of compassion within your heart. It's being able to reconcile your needs and fears and insecurities so that you can become bigger and have energy left over for the benefit of others. It's a form of tithing on an energy level. You say to yourself, *I am silently big, so I have energy to give away*. That's your affirmation.

In our modern society, people are small and insecure. They have little time for others. How often have you been in conversations with friends, and they are just yakking on about their life, their acquisitions, their job, their feelings, their relationships? You can see that they are self-obsessed. A part of developing this spirituality within you so that your sixth sense can grow is developing a magnanimous goodness within you that supports others with kindness and compassion. It is by being kind and supportive and loving that you reach the ultimate God force within you.

The God force is the most kick-ass sixth-sense tool you have ever seen. A few dollops of that force and you will be the wizard on the mount pronto.

When you are with friends, as a part of your ever-developing perception and sensuality, rather than talking, become a listener, ask questions, and ask questions that you want to hear the answers to. Don't just ask out of politeness. Make it a discipline that when you ask them a question that you look them in the eye, and you are there with them, heart chakra to heart chakra. You are there inside their humanity, watching their eyes, watching their lips move, watching their expressions, while they are talking about their fishing trip, for example. Now the story of their fishing trip might be a long and winding bore, but it's part of your discipline to listen. It's a part of your discipline to be loving and compassionate. And it's a part of your discipline to be there for others.

In the act of service and the act of being there for people, you come inside that sense of all knowing, that sense of spirituality in all things. It's an affirmation that says you are the wizard; you are not short of energy, or money or ideas, or generosity or anything else. You have an oversupply of everything at your fingertips. Even if right now things may be a little tight or a little thin on the ground, no matter the reality, there's a mind-boggling amount of everything out there, and you are a part of it. You are in line waiting to step up and collect. Most cut themselves off from the power because they are too deeply inside the ego, too deeply inside their own fears and their own pain. They are too mean and too small and too sick to be infinite.

It's fashionable these days for everybody to be in some kind of childhood pain, or past life pain, or other kinds of pain. They have been abused or they have been used or some painful thing has been happening to them. And as soon as you sit down next to them, you know they are going to take the next hour to tell you all about their pain. Of course, it's a good thing for people to release their pain, but in our society, there aren't enough listeners.

There seems to be more pain to people than there are happy listeners. Get shot of your pain pronto. These emotions wreck your etheric, and that stuffs up your perception. It forces you to dive down a hole within yourself—one that is often self-indulgent. You can't see properly if you're in a hole.

The simplest and easiest way to go beyond your pain is by working on and concentrating on your strengths. I know psychologists will tell you that you have to take your wounds. Take your inner child and the various psychological factors within you to a therapist who will help you identify them, and then you have to live them out or release them.

There is nothing wrong with that system. But it has its drawbacks. By judging it all up and talking about it, the ego rises up because it's being noticed, and it focuses on the injustice of it all. The ego hops onto its righteous soapbox and beats its little chest calling for attention and sympathizers: *Look at me, what a horrible life I have had. I need help and care and specialness, and I need attention, and everyone should commiserate with me and cut me a lot of slack.*

It's hard to get rid of your past experiences when you have to dredge them up twice weekly for the therapist.

That takes years and lots of moolah and it stops you going forward at any decent speed. So you regress to the dimension or the time frame when things happened to you in the past. You stall your evolution by treading water as you become locked in a time warp for as long as it takes. Time passes, and all you are doing is dis-ease. You grow old, and love affairs and experiences and opportunities go elsewhere because you're in a smoky fugue of your own. You will come back later, much later, like the next incarnation or maybe the one after that. Maybe you will be ready for new opportunities then. Right now you are too busy with all this old stuff.

There is a simpler way.

That simpler way is developing serenity within, detaching and working on your strengths. Bit by bit, the pain of your life goes away. Of course, you have to remember that we didn't come here for a perfect life. I wish we did, but we didn't. We didn't come for physical, emotional, spiritual, and mental perfection. Each one of us was given something we had to go beyond. And that is the nature of this journey—working upon yourself continually to reach the Holy Grail within. You will get there.

Take time to meditate and notice the things that caused you pain in the past. And then release them and concentrate on your strengths. The more equitable you get with yourself, the more you will be in touch with the yin and the softness, and it is there that you will find your creative talent, whether your interest is film, acting, painting, computer programming, sports, or whatever. It's in the softness of the creative subconscious self that one touches back into the God force, and the collective unconscious wherein dwells the all knowing—stepping back within and knowing and believing that anything is possible.

As you begin to come from that magnanimous creative self, then you are going to start to think in terms of the subtlety of who you are. It's not just an issue of how you will make ends meet, and how you will vibrate an extrasensory power, but you will also start thinking in terms of how you will serve humanity.

As part of the sacred journey, each one of us has to take time out and serve. We can't just live in a world of self-aggrandizement, money making, and issues of self. We have to serve in order to understand ourselves in this evolution, and to come to some kind of fruition inside this evolution.

In the last chapter, I discussed having the courage to claim your power, to create limitless expectations, and follow through. Here, I want to discuss defining your purpose in life. Before you can offer something valuable to the world, as I suggested earlier, you have to reconcile yourself. You have to understand the God force flowing through you, the life force wherein the inner knowing exists. Once you understand that concept of inner knowing, you can have whatever you want.

What are your goals? If you don't know what you want, I think it's important that you start to pray to the God force, Jesus, or your higher power and ask that it show you a being that is wandering around without knowing what they want like a ship without a rudder. It's impossible when you don't know what you want. What you want may not be anything terribly grandiose. It may just be serenity, freedom from money worries, a healthy body, and enough time off to enjoy the mountains. But you have to decide because in defining your life, you create the power.

I think a purpose in life, however, that doesn't include serving other people isn't worth having. You should decide how you will serve. If you have served, did you serve well? Did you serve the God force? Or was it a big ego trip? Once you have decided what you are going to do, then already you stand inside a control mechanism that says, *Even though I don't know all the answers, even though I can't see everything, I believe that my life is in order, that it is divinely guided, divinely led.* Of course, you are divinely led, because you can touch into the Christ consciousness, the collective unconscious, anytime you reach into the sacred silence within.

As I said before, you breathe in and you see yourself in that eternal stance traveling at an infinite velocity.

These perceptions are important. And even though you might have looked at them before, now is the time to look at them again. As ideas and concepts come around over and over and each time they show you something that you didn't see last time, that's the cute part of it all.

Let me now go into the various aspects of the sixth sense in more detail. As I said at the beginning, the sixth sense divides into three main categories. And then there are several subcategories. The main components are the intuitive sixth sense, the psychic sixth sense, and the all-knowing sixth sense.

First, let's look at psychic powers. Psychic energy is fleeting. That's because it is in its common form telepathy. You can't button down telepathy, but it's something that we all practice from time to time without really being aware of it. It is especially strong between people who know each other well, such as spouses, family members, and good friends.

Telepathy isn't rare. Think how often you have been thinking about something totally out in left field. And the person next to you mentioned exactly the same idea. How can that happen? A small part of it may be coincidence, but that doesn't explain how thoughts seem to jump across from two separate people. It happens a million times a day around the world—thoughts jump, so either you got the thought from the person sitting next to you, or they got it from you, or you both got it from someone else like a passerby.

Nonetheless, the thought you had jumped across the space between you and the person next to you and you both thought the same thing. The psychic reader or spirit medium may use a tool like a crystal or tarot card to help the process along, but the person still has to be picking up thoughts and feelings that have jumped.

I am not belittling a psychic process in any way. The information may be very useful to you. It's just defining how it's done. Now some of the psychic readers' perceptions come out of a good sense of understanding people. When you can really look at people and notice them, there is a whole bunch of information they tell you without ever opening their mouth. A reader, for example, may see struggle written all over their customer's face. And the psychic may say, "Your life has been hard, and you need a special person in your life to give you a bit of support and help and you deserve a bit more money, don't you?"

And the customer says, "Yes, yes, yes, how did you know? Amazing!"

That's experience. It comes from knowing people. I will talk about reading people like a book in the next chapter. Meanwhile, let's stick with intuition and the psychic faculty, so we know how they work. Intuition is slightly different to the psychic faculty as intuition is often the appearance of subliminal information that comes from your mind. Let's say you will think, *I have got a gut feeling this project will work.* Where did that gut feeling come from? As often as not, it comes from all the subliminal information you have picked up about the project as you have gone along.

Subliminal means below the normal threshold of conscious awareness. We pick up much more in life than we are immediately aware of. So you may have gotten a load of information from the people involved. That subtlety told you things about their attitude. It gave you subliminal information that you picked up at a business meeting, for example. Later your subconscious sorts out that hidden information, and in a quiet moment, it pops into your mind as a hunch, or a strange thought that doesn't seem to connect to your current conscious stream of thinking. You seem to know things that logically your intellect shouldn't know.

Intuition, then, is often the ability to delve deep into your subconscious mind and pull out all the information you have accumulated, not just the information you intellectually sorted out as being the most important, but all the other information as well.

It's a bit like going to the races. The racing form might say that horse number one, Acer Racer, will win hands down. But as you look at the horse, you know it won't, and that, in fact, horse number two, Johnny Rocket, is the best bet. How do you know?

Well, intellectually, you should back Acer Racer. But subliminally you have picked up that Acer isn't looking too swift and you subliminally heard the trainer who is 40 yards away tell the stable boy that Acer was feeling a bit worse for wear, as it had banged its shin in the horsebox. And subliminally you read the face of Acer's jockey. He looked bored as he walked up to the horse and seemed to have other things on his mind, like the cute stable girl that's leading good old Johnny Rocket round the paddock.

Suddenly, you have a strong intuition Johnny Rocket is going to win it. Intellectually, you don't know how you know, as your conscious mind is not normally in direct communication with your subconscious where subliminal information is stored. So intuition is more often than not your subconscious showing you things in a quiet moment when your intellect has stopped waffling on.

The subconscious is showing you what it has picked up—what either you have forgotten, or what you picked up subliminally and you are not aware of. This type of intuition or perception comes forward as you quiet your emotions, as you go within meditating and accessing the subconscious via dreams and visions.

Sometimes the universe at large talks to you especially when there is a need at a synchronistic moment. You ask a question or something happens by chance at that very moment to answer your question, or someone unrelated to the situation or the question you have asked answers it for you at that very instant. Let me give you an example.

I was at Newton Abbot Racecourse one day—a small course in the west of England. I had been tanking back a few beers and hadn't really been concentrating. And it was now the last race and I was about 1,000 pounds down on the day. And I suddenly realized that if I didn't get my act together, I would walk away losing money. And that's against my religion. I am very sanctimonious when it comes to taking money off the guys who make the book (bookies).

Anyway, it was a slushy day and it was a National Hunt meet, meaning that horses raced over jumps, which were wet and unpredictable. I was in a private box boozing with some racing buddies, and as I was pondering the last race, in walks England's number one champion trainer. With him is England's most winning jockey, Peter Scudamore. He had been champion jockey over the jumps each year, every year, as far back as anyone could remember.

So I asked the trainer whose name was Martin, "I say, Martin, what's going to win the last race?" He says number one. I can't remember the horse's name, but let's say it was Acer Racer once more. Sure enough, the champion jock tells me that, barring accidents, Acer is a good bet.

So I was off to the bookies with a view to plunging 1,000 on Acer at about even money. Meaning if it won, I would get my 1,000 pounds plus my stake back. Now I was standing in front of the fat bookie about to make my bet, but something in my feelings was worrying me. I was not sure about Acer Racer. I always operate from the old axiom that says, "If you don't know, don't go." So I took a meditative moment, clutching my last 1,000 pounds wondering. I asked the universe at large what horse was going to win this next race. And as I asked, I looked up and I saw the bookie was talking to a customer who pointed to number two on his board—good old Johnny Rocket. I took that as a sign, when another fellow came past me and he said to a friend in quite a loud voice that I could hear, "I am on Johnny Rocket." He said, "I don't fancy that Acer Racer, it worries me."

Acer Racer worried me, too, so I decided to plunge 500 on Johnny Rocket at four to one. During the race, Acer Racer and Johnny Rocket were coming up the home stretch, neck and neck miles ahead of the others. But at 300 yards I knew, I absolutely knew, Acer wouldn't make it. And sure enough, 100 yards from home, Johnny Rocket pulled ahead and won by half a length. So I won two grand on that race and got my stake back.

When I returned to the box, the trainer said he was sorry that he led me astray over Acer Racer and that he would try harder next time. I told him how I listened carefully to his advice, but that I changed my mind at the last moment and bet Johnny Rocket instead. He asked me how I knew. I told him it was a lucky guess.

I didn't mention how seconds before the race started the universe at large knew which horse was going to win. And in certain circumstances, the universe talks to you if you settle down and listen, and if you are in the right spot in the right moment, and if you have no fears, and if you can read the signs and plunge into your beliefs and back your fleeting visions and impressions and so forth. I didn't tell the trainer that stuff.

What you know in life about the power, you keep to yourself unless people ask you or unless they indicate in some way that they are interested in what you have to say. You should never infringe on others by giving them information about themselves or their situations if they haven't asked for it. Each has his or her evolution, their own path through life. And it's wrong to dive in and try to change that or to try to come off as a god and pronounce what their directions should be. You should disturb things as little as possible, and let everyone head off in whatever direction they choose—even if you know they are choosing a long and winding path. Maybe they need to bet 1,000 on Acer Racer. Who knows?

7

Archetypes to Develop Your Sixth Sense

Everyone is inside the one global mind, and that global mind is segmented into obvious categories.

Once you know and understand people, life gets easier. And the sixth-sense perception flows more and more. When it comes to people, there are only about a total of ten life stories in the whole world. And each archetype has its own very obvious characteristics. Of course, everyone has individual traits, and an individual story. But the generalizations are true, as everyone is inside the one global mind, and that global mind is segmented into obvious categories.

As a part of developing perception, you can start to slot people you see in the street or wherever you see people into the categories I am about to give you. It helps you understand their issues, and you pick up psychic tidbits off their mind. It is loads of fun and good practice. It helps your perception.

Here is the main cast of characters in no particular order. You will spot them from among your family and friends. Once you have the categories under your belt, everything else drops into place, and, *bingo*, people become obvious.

Troubled Youth

The first character is called the troubled youth. They are usually under thirty or perhaps they are over thirty and they never grew up. This archetype is called the Peter Pan syndrome, where a mature person still acts like a child, or they cling to their parents and never get out into real life. The young version of the troubled youth needs acceptance and direction. They are anti-everything because they can't accept themselves and their circumstances. They don't have an identity.

Sometimes this happened because they were enmeshed with their parents. And sometimes it happened because of abuse in childhood. Sometimes they just mixed up. Troubled as they are, they play a game of chicken like jumping in front of trains. They are saying, *Hey world, if you don't stop what you are doing and attend to me and notice me and help me, I will self-destruct, and then it will be your fault and you will be sorry.*

In quantum physics, subatomic particles exist in a wave state with no particular defined position or solidity. It is known as the hazy wave. When you concentrate on a particle, it changes at a quantum level. It moves from a hazy ill-defined wave state where it exists in potentially nowhere to a particular state. The particle changes by the act of your watching it, and suddenly it becomes solid. It has validity and the definite location—gone is the hazy state. All this happens just because someone is observing the particle. Weird! But scientifically true.

People are the same. If you want to perceive and understand and perhaps heal the troubled youth, notice them, take them from hazy wave to particle, and make them solid. After all, they need identity. That's why they have colored their hair lime green and puce just so you will notice. So take time to notice. Don't judge them for being a twit. They will run away. Notice and try not to giggle at the chopstick they stuck through their nose. Just notice. Simple healing.

Once you notice the troubled youth, they feel more secure. They are only out of control because they need to be noticed. Give them what they want. Build them up, endorse them. Once you secure them, they will find direction and meaning and won't self-destruct. Why do you think so many young people straighten up once they find a romantic partner? Because if the partner is solid and not bouncing off the walls like they are, then the troubled youth has someone attentive to notice them. So they heal.

Rabbit

The rabbit is scared. There are lots of rabbits in the world. They can't handle life. They are paralyzed by fear and in a shell. They may be very bright and so they hide behind the intellectuality and tootle around with their internet or whatever. But the rabbit doesn't like to come out of its hole and experience life.

Deep within, the rabbit is often a bit angry. Life is passing them by. Also, the rabbit is full of injustices. They need encouragement and endorsement to feel secure enough to come out of their hole so tell the rabbit what they want to hear. Tell them it's safe to come out and offer to take a little walk and help them along. Etherically, the rabbit is easy to spot as their energy stops close to their body. They aren't out there booming, expressing themselves outwardly connected to life. Their energy peters out close to their body and looks weak. It does not express itself well.

The wilting wallflower is another version of the rabbit. The wallflower uses their weakness as a come-on. They need people to rescue them. They are looking for a white knight. Don't buy it, unless you are into hauling a dead horse through life. Well, sooner or later you will resent it. Instead, try to get them to empower themselves, help them out of their timidness and shyness, and teach them not to use weakness in a covert and sneaky way.

Tyrant

The tyrant is so angry, usually because they are scared. But more often than not, they are tyrants because they were abused as kids. Sometimes they are angry because they feel they haven't had the breaks in life that they think they ought to have had. So they project their needs onto others. It's an insecurity thing. They desperately need to be loved. They live in an emotional desert because no one likes them and that makes them even more miserable and insecure. These people project that insecurity on others and become the military tyrant, or the domineering father who never thought anything was ever good enough. Or they are the emotionally tyrannical mother who is hard to control and dominates the family through the use of emotion and theatrics.

The tyrant, more often than not, is a nobody and often a failure, so they need someone else to fill the gap of their inadequacy. Therefore, the tyrant places unreasonable demands on others, dominating and controlling them to bolster themselves up, to assist them with their fears and insecurities. Meanwhile, they spread fear and terror, and they control with emotion, violence, and threats.

If you don't have a PhD in psychology and lots of time to spare, stay away from the tyrants. If you have to deal with a tyrant, remember this: even though they are desperately unhappy, they become arrogant and dogmatic through the exercise of their tyranny. You will very rarely get a tyrant to see reason because they live in their own rabid empire. They are fascists basically. Try not to deal with the tyrants. But if you have to, remember this: tyrants like and expect abuse. Don't negotiate, don't accommodate. Don't try to please them. For the more you do, the more they will want of you. Don't cut these suckers any slack.

They are the schoolyard bully who won't back off till they get a punch on the nose. Don't try to change them. And don't try to keep them happy. Just whack them on the head with the biggest psychological, contractual, emotional, or financial plank you have got. And when and if they get up, then whack them one more time for good measure. They expect it and they will respect you and cause less trouble.

Over the years I have tried love and kindness and reason with this sort and it works sometimes. But I find walking away is the best move and a whack on head is the second best move. The tyrant is sometimes hard to spot, as often they cloud that tyranny covertly by feigning reasonableness. But you can usually spot them from their expression as it's hard to hide all the anger and violence that they project.

Widow

The widow (male or female) may never have actually been married, but they are often married to an idea. And the idea died. So that's why I call them the widow because they have suffered a bereavement. The widow has a vacant expression and they are uncomfortable and lack direction. They suffer because often a cherished idea that they held onto has disappeared or passed on. The idea was all that they had in life. Sometimes the idea was a situation that they were used to, and that died or changed or disappeared in some way.

The widow type is typically thirty-five to fifty-five years old. Their dreams fell apart, or they were unrealistic about them, or they suffered from fear or they never had the energy to pull it off. Sometimes the widow type just had bad luck. And they got put off their dream. They didn't dig deep enough when things got tough. So now they are drifting. The widow always needs an impossibly big break. As their currency, their energies lowering all the time, it's hard for that break to define them, for they are concentrating on grieving on what they haven't got, instead of going for something new and fresh.

In addition, their energy falls flat because they feel defeated or lost. It's not that they don't have anything to offer, it's just that they are stuck. Their loss may have caused them to feel weak and insecure.

Here's a solution: Tell them that they are great, and that there is a lot to live for. And get them to set aside the old dream and to reconcile it in their psychology and to acknowledge what they do have and to go out and meet new people and come up with some new ideas and fall in love and get laid and go crazy a bit and dance all night. Get out of all the old stuff and all the dusty ideas and try something new, anything.

I used to tell the middle-aged types that came to my seminars that fitted into this widow category to go out and bonk a stranger and get drunk. They would be terribly shocked. But their eyes would light up, and then I would tell them that I didn't really expect them to be quite that radical. But they should at least get their party frocks on and pitch up Saturday night to the big bash, looking good.

Here is what you tell the widows: Hang out with young people more. Tell them to hang out with creators and inventors and innovators and bright characters that are doing things. And tell them to pick up any loose threads of creative ideas that they might have set aside in the past. Ask them to start reading more and searching and tell them to go to the mountains and don't forget to party.

The widow needs to pamper themselves and acknowledge their trauma and realize that they have a lot to offer and that life is open and wide and big. There's a lot of time ahead. The widow type is sad and labored by old stuff. They only need permission from someone in authority, and they will be gone to a new exciting life. So give them permission, turn them into the merry widow. Take them dancing, skinny dipping in the lake, drinking a little too much, sleeping on the beach, whatever.

There is a variation of the widow. It's the Rip Van Winkle type. Here, they have been asleep for thirty years. They weren't alive or having fun even in the old days. They have come to Earth this time to have a good nap. Let them be; give them an extra pillow.

Priest

The priest as a category will not necessarily be in any religious order, but they think they are. They are very righteous and very holy moly. Priests in this sense often suffer from an inferiority complex that they cover over by deciding that they have been chosen personally by God to haul everybody to the Promised Land.

You have to watch this lot for quite often they will have a magazine they want you to read or something they want you to join, or they want you to buy some holy something that you don't want. They may try to get you on the green slime tofu diet. Or even worse, they might try to get you to read a thousand-page book by some obscure Indian from the Hindu Kush that puts people to sleep for a living.

The priest and priestess aren't any real trouble, though they need to feel superior and chosen and special, because they don't like themselves. They need acceptance, so accept them. Tell them you love them. Tell them not to take it personally when you say you don't want the green slime at an exorbitant price for a little bottle. The priests are a bit weird. But one day they will love and accept themselves. They will throw away their robes and come back to the real world. Or they won't.

Terrorist

These people have usually been disadvantaged in life, and they won't fit in no matter what. Anytime they get near to success, they will self-destruct and cause a scene, or they will join an organization but not be a supporter. The terrorist really wants to destroy the place. They will feel judged in any way it goes against their terrorist philosophy. So rather than joining in, they will figure a way to shoot themselves in the foot rather than bending a bit to make it in life.

The terrorist needs to know they are okay. They need to know it doesn't matter if they are not socially acceptable, as they can make themselves acceptable by just accepting himself or herself. Also, once the terrorist sees how they hurt their cause, they will often change their ways. But deep within they really want success, money, and to belong. Deep within, the terrorist really wants to be accepted and to join in and to have status. They are desperate for it.

Once the terrorist's desire for success is stronger than their conflict about not being accepted, then they will ease back and be reasonable and hang in there long enough to step up and collect. So tell them they are okay and offer them status. Show them how to feel good about themselves and show them that it's more sensible to put aside one's ego and one's issues rather than fight all the way. Get them to realize they have to put their issues to one side long enough anyway to collect the prize.

Professional Victim

The professional victim is really the wilting wallflower in another disguise. They have been victimized or they think they have been, even if they haven't, not any more than anyone else anyway. They still like to make life into a substory, a tragic opera. Often they will hire someone to help them sort out the story. They might embellish it and wind it up and make a huge fuss of it. They aren't too strong and they need attention. They have got a hangdog energy.

It's easy to see in the etheric as it turns in on itself curved over like an ingrown toenail. Trouble comes and finds this character. They become accident prone because etherically they are sucking energy from outside of themselves, pulling it into them from anything or anyone that might lend support to a hopeless case. That opens them up to a lot of grungy stuff. Often the victim is a little bit self-indulgent. They want someone to hold them up, to provide for them, to save them. And they don't want to do that much to heal themselves, other than to tell their story and moan and groan and blame the world.

Much like the widow, you have to get the victim to move from their injustices and to open up and try new things. It isn't easy to persuade them, as a victim has a vested agenda in their story. It's an asset that gets some attention and makes them feel special. So the story is valuable to them. You have to try to get them to see that their story is just that, a story. It's a tale of a human experience, as seen from one person's eyes, and often it may be slanted to one side ignoring all the other directions, especially the exit.

The victim type can be a bit grim, as they are vacuum cleaners. You know them, you have chatted with them for a few minutes in the supermarket, and they want you out, energy-wise. They suck on you and pull from your energy. They need your life force because their etheric is turned inward. It's not out there expressing itself and keeping them safe. Their energy is a bit limp, it feels unstable, and so they are very needy. They won't let you go until they have got every drop of your power, and you are on your knees exhausted. At that point, they are a bit happier and they trot off to find another sucker to fill up from.

You have to protect yourself psychically from the professional victim. Avoid close body contact because etheric energy jumps. When you are talking to them, keep your distance at least 18 inches; if you can manage 18 miles, so much the better. The way to deal with them is to be compassionate but to keep offering them the solution. It doesn't matter if the solution you are offering makes no real sense to them or if they will never act upon your idea. Keep offering the solution all the same. Make one up if you have to. Offer the solution but don't buy the emotion, that's fatal. You will get sucked in.

If you offer too much sympathy and free energy, they will move in. They will eat your lunch, energy-wise and literally. Sure you can help a friend who is a bit low, but that's a whole different thing to becoming a paramedic for basket cases, isn't it?

Keep offering the solution, don't buy the emotion, and one or two things will happen. Either the professional victim will take your advice and go fix their life. That doesn't happen that often. Or they get very little joy from hearing you tell them the sensible answer because that means they have to drop the story and get off their stuff. They will eventually wander off and find or pay someone else to buy the emotion. They need sympathizers and listeners, people who think life is a bowl of sludge and hard and painful and thick and gummy—a bit like their brain.

Saviors or Supreme Achievers

And then there's the supreme achiever, the saviors. In a way these characters are quite cool and fun to be with, as they usually have great stories. They have done things in life. They are usually natural-born leaders and they carry the whole tribe on their shoulders. They are responsible for everything, and they will go out in the rain at three in the morning to shut the shed door that's banging in the wind. Of course they do all that stuff because they are sacrificial. They are like martyrs and want everyone to admire them for their courage.

They like to be acknowledged for their service to humanity. They are hoping for prizes in shed door shuttings, and even if you are prepared to grant them such accolades, they would never stick around to collect the medal, because accepting praise and acknowledgment is contrary to the sacrificial lamb energy that forms a part of their psychology. Instead, the saviors aspire to a life to save everyone in the village and then ride out of town so everyone can say, "Wow, what a great guy. Who was that masked stranger?"

These supreme achievers are usually children of wimpy parents who expected a lot, so the child had to overcompensate and win at everything, to be very competitive, and show Daddy and Mummy and the rest of the world that they are okay. You want to be careful of this nonsense as it kills you quickly.

The supreme achievers are easy to spot. They have a booming energy, but it's not usually contained and disciplined. Instead, it's usually billowing out in every direction, folding over the top of people, swamping them more often than not. People like this type around but not for too long. Once they have done all the work and provided all the money and sacrificed themselves, you tire of them quickly. The supreme achiever takes your breath away. They are like an overly long kiss you are sort of enjoying for a bit anyway, but after a while you start thinking you are going to pass out for lack of air.

Because of the supreme achiever's booming etheric energy, they will always feel ripped off. Why is that? Well, the achiever booms because they need followers, people to accept them, people to admire their many and various achievements. So they spray out energy, flashing across the sky like a shooting star, and everyone is lit up by their presence. But then they are wiped out and have no energy left, and everybody takes what they need and more.

Not satisfied with any amount of money or fame or glamour, achievement or assets or toys, the savior always goes for more. And though they help people out of a kind heart, and from their booming energy, they also do it to satisfy their own agenda, as they don't think much of themselves.

Suffering Servant

Once upon a time, there was a little girl who didn't feel loved and perhaps she wasn't loved by her parents. And because she didn't feel loved, she felt inadequate. She grew to feel she owed the world a favor, so she started dishing out favors. Sad, really, it felt safe to her. She prostituted herself to win acceptance and feel better. She didn't want to have to take responsibility and she didn't want to stick out in a crowd or amount to very much. Instead, she could latch onto strong people and tag along with them.

She served them and they used her and she will go to bed at night well pleased with herself and righteous to boot. She would be doing an impersonation of a doormat. She would say to herself, *I am the humble doormat, doormat is safe. God loves doormats, and he is saving a special place for them in heaven. It says so somewhere doesn't it?*

Truth be known, God doesn't treat doormats any differently to anyone else in that the God force just reflects impartially back to you what you are. If you are a doormat, and you wind up at the pearly gates in the suffering servant mode, then the first thing you will see are the letters EMOCLEW shining back at you. And you will wonder and scratch your head, *What in heaven's name is that?*

Suddenly you realize that you are looking at the mirror image of a welcome mat: WELCOME. You don't want to be an EMOCLEW, as that's not *looc*, I mean cool. EMOCLEWs of etheric energy say, *Use me, plow over me, treat me like a fool, treat me mean and cruel. And when you have had your fill, pass me on to someone else who will also treat me badly. In that way I can make amends and feel useful.*

When healing the suffering servant, you have to get them to see that being of service to others is a wonderful thing. But they can't give themselves away totally within that service. They have to love and accept themselves, but they can't compromise just to feel safe, to be accepted, and to give their life meaning. There is nothing meaningful about a doormat that everybody wipes their life on.

Boffin

Ah, they think a lot and when they are finished thinking about what they just thought of, they start right back at the beginning to think it all through one more time. And when they have finished that, they wonder if they have missed anything and so they go back and start over. Boffins make their brains a God and eventually they become convinced that their mind is God. But in the end, they run out of things to think about. Sadly, they often live hollow lives thinking about the same stuff.

Churning through all the thoughts they have had a million times before, they lose a connection with the earth and with life. In effect, they decapitate themselves. Their head separates from their heart. They lose sight of compassion for themselves and others that makes them miserable. They become critical and antagonistic. Often they want others to agree with the idea that their mind is God, and they get very upset when people won't cooperate.

The problem with overthinking is that you lose touch with sensitivity in life. It makes you neurotic, and your head and heart separate to float off in different directions. So you lose touch with where life really exists. Eventually, your brain falls off its perch and hits ground zero—a bit like the French Revolution, really. The elite in France were way too far into their heads, and they viewed themselves a bit too pompous. They lost a connection with compassion, with their heart. The people of France, the spirit of the French tribal soul, pondered what to do.

Eventually, it felt the simplest solution was to cut off its head and allow the heart to grow and emotion to flow. So they tried that one Monday morning, as it was raining as I recall, loads of heads and emotion flowed all over the place, and the spirit of France felt a bit better. The French heart did grow a bit, and the French became even more exotic, which is nice.

If you are a boffin and you have lost your connection to your heart, then you better discipline your mind to back off and shut up and you better go find your heart and play with children and be happy and funny and not too serious. You better put a time lock on your computer and your books and all that dusty stuff. You should run barefoot in the desert and love the little things of life and be kind and stay on the ground and be human and don't make your intellect a god. Try to love people and not judge them and try to love the God force as best you can.

We all suffer from overthinking. But for some it creates great turmoil and pain, indecision and confusion. I have often said that confusion comes from questions. You can't be confused if you don't ask questions, or confusion starts with a question such as *Shall I? Will I? Won't I?* You can't reach God through your mind. You have to touch the God force in your feelings in a million places—in nature, in people's eyes, in the loveliness of the sunset, and so forth.

Overthinking destroys your perception because it blurs your feelings, and it makes it impossible to visualize, to vision, and to dream. And if you can't vision and see and dream, you are stuffed, doggedly stuffed. So push the mind back when it worries and bitches and say, *I will handle that later, we will talk later.* Then deliberately avoid mentioning the subject again.

When the mind is neurotic, take it for a three-mile run and throw it into a freezing lake at five in the morning. Better still, engage in helping others do things that are useful and that exist outside in the external world beyond mental churning. And when the mind wants things incessantly, tell it, *Tough, Ducky, tough. My higher power is in control here.*

When it drives you crackers and gets you into turmoil with other people and it battles on for days on end, stop eating. Try that for three days. If it's still grumbling and arguing, then don't eat for two or three more days, as long as it takes for the mind to shut up. The mind goes quiet when you don't eat. It takes it personally, sits down in a corner, and quits.

In the end, too much thinking kills you because, as the mind runs out of power, it turns to worrying about death. The more it thinks of death, the more death trots up to it saying, *Ahh . . . another customer a real brain box. They will be finished early.* Feel the exuberance of life, join the sensuality of it, be in it, dance and play and perceive what there is to perceive and be light-hearted and carefree. Don't be pompous and serious. Allow life to flow and allow your infinite self to teach you things you can't find in books. Loosen up and party down and go with the flow as much as you can. Make sure you get out into the mountains or by the sea or in the desert as often as possible. That's where life is. That's where the heart is. That's where perception lies.

Mountain-man Jack and his wilderness-woman Jill

Now mountain-man Jack and his girl bought a couple of plaid shirts from L.L. Bean. They got in the pickup and went up the hill and stayed there. They're real earthy, and you can see them coming a mile off. It's like they've got carrots in their aura. I like Jack because he's not full of thinking and he knows simple stuff like when the rat mates and when it doesn't. Jack is easy to deal with. And he's usually quite humble and generous of spirit and close to God.

His lady is nice, too, and she makes pots and weaves things and grows veggies and she's got a heart. They are all-round simple people, and cool and easy to get on with. The only downside is that sometimes the mountain types are real loners. They cut themselves off from people. Sometimes they even get angry because they don't like people spoiling the environment, because living out in the middle of nowhere as they do, they often suffer a few financial problems.

You almost never see the mountain-man Jack type in therapy because when he gets pissed off, he goes walk about. He processes his feelings through nature and hard work like chopping wood and carrying water and stuff that he has to do to survive. But his natural spirituality is in nature, not in his head. He passes his feelings through nature, where they are processed and absorbed by it. He's in touch with his nature self as we all should be. And he's got it right.

We urban types have got it wrong, for the most part. Go hang out with that dude and his lady and sit in the dirt by a little fire and have her tell you about how the streams flow. Listen when he tells you about what coyotes sniff and what they don't like to sniff and sit there and watch the stars and think about the galaxies under your feet and flick your energy to the end of the universe and back and drink a little tea. Jill will have a nice bowl of veggies gurgling away in one of her pots and you will remember things.

You will remember what God is and you will remember what life is really about. You will perceive and you will see the sixth sense working through your nature self and you will see the infinity within you. What you won't think about is dysfunction and trouble.

*   *   *

As you are watching all the archetypal characters go past at the shopping mall, identify who fits into what category and see who might fit into more than one category. Who is the boffin? Some people you see are on the cusp, so to speak, like their moon is in struggle and their planets are in silliness.

Watching them, you learn to feel out what people's energy offers you, to find out their issues. Reach out mentally and tap the side of their head at the temple, like reaching out and extending an etheric arm and lightly tapping them on the side of the head and see what comes back to you. Maybe it's a word, maybe it's an impression. Usually that impression will be an emotion—their over-riding emotion.

8

Claim Your Power

If it feels wrong, it is wrong.

Have you ever seen a symbol flash up in your mind's eye? Or consider an occasion when your mind suddenly flips back to some period in your life. Let's say a little boy you haven't seen for twenty years comes back to mind. He's standing by the river the two of you used to play beside, and you wonder why you are thinking about him.

It's the subconscious's way of showing you that the character that is passing in front of you at the shopping mall (the technique from the previous chapter, viewing people as they pass by) is similar to or the same energy as the one that you associate with the little boy by the river many years ago. That's why you sometimes dream of school friends you haven't seen for years. It's the subconscious's language reminding you of feelings that were associated with people or events in the past like the time you put ice cream down Susie Whatnot's dress and she whacked you in the head with a school bag.

Sometimes the association is connected to a place rather than a person. It's usually a location that you know from the past that you associate with an emotion: a restaurant, perhaps, where you had a fight, a club where you met a beautiful person, an office where you concluded a money-making deal, for examples. Etherically tapping people as they pass, you make the connection so you get used to picking up stuff from people's minds and from their energy, their etheric, and their emotions. You expect to receive information. It's easy and natural. And it's what you do every time you meet new people and scope them out in an inner way. That's the feature of psychic power. It's a mental telepathy.

First and foremost, you pull information from the mind etheric, the personalities of others, picking up bits of information. Places have the same telltale energy. You can tell if a room is a happy, empowering place or if it's ugly and dangerous or negative. Here's a good mental setup.

Remember a building that you know that has high energy, maybe a beautiful church or cathedral or perhaps a room in your home or someone else's home. Perhaps you know of an art gallery that's very beautiful. Set that up in your mind and give it a rating of 10 points. Now contrast it by remembering a place you know that has a very low energy and unhappy negative energy. Set that up in your mind with a rating of just 1.

So now there is a spread in your perception from 1 to 10 that you can use to evaluate places energy-wise. Next time you go into a building or home, give the room or place you're in a rating compared to your preset scale of 1 to 10. Just ask and a number will flash into your mind. If the place is more or less neutral, it will be in the 5 to 6 range. If it scores higher, it's a nice place to be. Pull energy from that location, zing your mind out into space and back again, pause and reflect for a moment, and something might come off the energy of the place you're in. If the location scores 4 or less, then you shouldn't be there. If you have to be there, stay balanced and watch and be aware and make a special note of where the exits are.

Never go into a building or a deal or marriage or any situation in life without first looking for the exit. That's not the sixth sense. That's common sense. You can set up the same 1 to 10 scale for people you meet. Make the highest energy person you know the number 10 and the lowest energy person you know the 1 spot. There's your scale.

When you meet people for the first time, exercise your perception on them right away. The first thing that comes to your mind is always the right one. Later, your perception gets clouded by circumstances or by the knowledge you may have subsequently acquired. If a person's rating is low, vote with your feet. Don't be shy to leave when things are not right, or if the energy of a place feels wrong, or if a person feels odd and they rattle your sensitivity.

That is not to judge people and places too harshly. One shouldn't become too prissy. A place can be just right for others. But if it feels wrong, it is definitely wrong for you. Leave. There's no God-given law that says you have to suffer low energy people. Socially, we often feel the need to be polite and accommodate others. But one has to learn good boundaries so that one can control one's life and one's energy. At times you will have to make excuses and duck away. Or you will have to refuse an invitation.

If in the heat of the moment you've already said yes to a proposal, and later you feel it's wrong, or its energy has changed and you feel uncomfortable having to tell people you want to cancel, then start the conversation with just that by saying, "Look, Harry, I feel very uncomfortable saying this, but I can't come to dinner next week."

Start by admitting your discomfort. That allows you a lot of leeway. It shows you to be human. And people can empathize with that no matter how much you are wriggling to get out of a commitment. You have to follow your feelings if you want to build power and make a stronger energy for yourself.

Put these words on your fridge: *If it feels wrong, it is wrong*. Period. Full stop. Sometimes your feelings can be a bit confusing, and sometimes things that feel okay now an hour later change and they don't feel okay. That's because situations are fluid and changing and people's feelings change. Or you have changed and now it's later in the day and you feel different.

While the idea has been hanging in your head for too long, and it's gone stale in the meantime, the universe at large has kindly shown you over the last few hours what a crummy idea it is and what a nightmare it might turn out to be. That is, if you go to dinner with Harry next Friday night, and maybe Harry's intentions, which were honorable when he first asked you, have now changed and he's gone dark in relation to the invitation or whatever.

Put Harry up in your mind's eye, and instead of firing the bubble at him, just look and see what your first impression is. See how much light or dark he emits, like on your scale of 1 to 10. Where does he fit in? Has that changed since you last looked at him? It's dead easy. People can't hide their energy; there is no place to hide in the all-encompassing light of God force anyway.

Objects, like people and places, also have an energy. The detecting of that energy, as you probably know, is called psychometry. You will probably never need psychometry unless you are one of those people who helps the police find bodies and murderers and so forth. But if you don't do that work, I wouldn't sign up for it as a few that I've met that work professionally in that way have all gotten very stressed and sick. Often their lives have been threatened and they take on a lot of badass energy. It's not worth it in my view. But psychometry is worth trying out as it all helps with sensitivity.

Action Step: Go to an antique shop and pick up the various items there and see what they tell you. The trick is to first mentally slot yourself into the historic timeframe of the object. If you are handling a piece of Victorian jewelry, for example, try to slot your mind into the Victorian era and try to feel how Victorian emotions might have been expressed by the owner of the jewel. What was important to people then? What were their overall psychological characteristics? What were their issues?

You ask yourself these kinds of questions. In handling the object, the first impression that comes through is usually the most accurate, for, once again, the longer you mull it over, the more your intellect gets into the act trying to help you out, not very successfully usually. Imagined psychometry would be handy if you were an art dealer or an antiquarian of some kind, as it would help you identify fakes. It would certainly warn you that things were not quite right.

A crook might be able to perfectly fake a painting, even down to using the right paints and frames and canvases, but you can't fake 500 years of emotion and feelings that have gone into a picture. If, as you handle an antique, it feels dead on an energy level, it can't be as old as it is said to be.

You can use a variation of this same technique when thinking about a proposal. You just handle it in your mind rather than literally. If someone's offered you a deal or a proposal to be involved in something at a future date, imagine holding the circumstances in the palm of your hands, turn it over back and forth and handle it. What level of energy does it give off? How much light?

If the proposal handles badly in your hands, you can be sure it will be a very dull event, and that it won't have much energy for you. Also, this handling process is a convenient way of figuring out how you feel about a future event or a proposal that has been made to you. Perhaps the proposal is fine, and perhaps you have made an intellectual decision to accept but, deep in your feelings, the whole idea is tedious and boring, or downright grim. Then, as you handle the proposal and look at it in your hands, it will feel that way, especially if you have taken time to lower yourself into a meditative state prior to handling the idea.

It is hard to do this kind of mental psychometry from the brain speed of the active waking state—the brain speed of the intellect of 14 to 21 cycles per second—for you will automatically at that level engage the intellect. For the best results, you will want to quiet the brain mechanism and be at a meditative state of consciousness.

If you haven't got time to really lower your brain speed properly via whatever meditation techniques you use, then create a symbol in your mind that acts as a biofeedback mechanism for the brain that automatically lowers its speed of oscillation. You might use a couple of ways to do that.

In the first technique, I go back to a mental picture that I associate with serenity. I remember a mountain lake I know and imagine myself sitting there, levitating, hovering in the center of the lake, totally at peace, silent, surrounded by the water in the morning mist. As I engage that thought, that visualization, I can feel my brain speed clunking down a gear or two.

Next time you meditate, set up the same process in your mind and enforce it by thinking about your peaceful scene from time to time. Use your own scene, of course, but always use the same mental picture. And remember to reinforce it in your meditations in your quiet time. Start every meditation thinking about the lake and say, *This is serenity.* That way the brain knows and remembers.

The other technique that comes from various sources, like Silva Mind Control, is a technique of putting the tips of your thumb and first two fingers together every time you meditate. The three fingers touching becomes a biofeedback trigger for the brain, and it remembers or associates the action with a time when it was oscillating at a lower speed, like in a trance meditation, so the three fingers together signal to the brain to fire at a slower rate. Both of the two mechanisms—the three-finger technique and the peaceful lake—should be tucked into your ever-increasing inventory of handy perception techniques.

Talking to the Dead

Mediumship, as the process of talking to the dead is called, began in America in the late 1800s with the Fox sisters. However, it was taken up by the British and became quite an institution. The old-fashioned type of mediumship that talks with spirits of the dead is really not a part of modern times anymore.

But we do look to communicate with higher beings from another world, ghosts and spirits of the departed and things that go bump in the night. Such spirits and angels exist in dimensions that are oscillating faster than ours, dimensions of a higher wisdom, individuals that have our highest evolution at heart. I believe there are all sorts of guiding forces in the inner worlds that are not only lovingly guiding the spiritual traveler, but more importantly, they are beaming the God force or life force into our earthly dimension for healing and perception, and you can call on those loving energies in your meditations and prayers to assist you.

The modern channeling process is done like this: The channel pulls energy up from within themselves. Most of it comes from the kundalini, the yogic life force said to be held at the base of the spine. Some of the energy comes from the compression of the channel, from the heart chakra, and the channel also pulls energy from the ambience, the setting, or the people present. The energy is pulled up consciously or unconsciously from the highest chakra up to the third eye chakra, and the channel uses the power to communicate.

Channeling is okay, but the problem I have with the old-fashioned mediumship is that the dead spirits that are supposed to be talking, making predictions, giving advice and so on, often seem to have such a limited knowledge of what is going on in the world today. In fact, they seem to have a limited understanding of life. They will tell you loads of very mundane stuff about how your granny is just hunky dory in the spirit world and that you will meet a tall dark stranger probably from the tax office, and things will be getting better for you given a month or two or ten or whenever.

I'm sure this stuff elevates people. Well, I know it does. I've seen them react. Sometimes the medium is very accurate, and they will say that they are communicating with your dad and then they will tell you some personal thing that only you and your dead relative would know, which helps convince some people that their parents really are alive in some other dimension.

First, I'm convinced that spirit worlds do exist, but I have come to that conclusion, not from spiritualism or mediumship, but by having had what are in effect experiences similar to those reported by people that have had near-death experiences. I became proficient at meditating, and eventually I could really charge myself down to a catatonic state without falling asleep or losing my awareness.

At this level of brain state, I have seen the tube that people say connects us to the celestial worlds, and I have had many, albeit short, glimpses of other dimensions. Therefore, I have come to believe in them.

However, I cannot say if the spirit medium is actually talking to your dead granny or not. The medium may be pulling off the person's thought forms just as easily as the medium might be telepathically communicating with a spirit entity that has departed the Earth plane. Whether it's real or not doesn't matter, does it? As long as it's helpful, and it pleases people and does do a bit of good.

I must say, having trained as a spirit medium years ago, I was very convinced about the presence of other entities at séances and so on. *Séances* is a French term. It comes originally from the Latin word *sedere* or to sit. In the séances that I was a part of, you really could feel the energy of the room change, and a flood of symbols and words came into your mind from left field, so to speak, and suddenly you might see a pig in your mind's eye, and you tell the person sitting with you, I have got your dad here, and he's showing me his prize pig. And the sitter confirms her dad was a pig farmer, and so on.

Here is what I think happens. I believe that when we incarnate into the Earth plane, we descend from some rarefied spirit evolution, we descend into close proximity to the feelings and thought forms of the Earth, that dimension of thought evolution that we call human. After we finish this incarnation, we move out of the physical molecule that we walked around in, so to speak, the physical body, into a side dimension or nearby dimension. And that spirit dimension is not very different to what we already know, in that it is close in feelings and ambience to the life when you were on Earth.

However, in the sight of the light of God, your personal identity melts. You become less and less Joe Smith, the pig farmer, and more and more infinite, more part of the Christ consciousness, the divine light—pick whatever term you want to call it. Once you have adjusted to the divine light all around you, you drift up and out of the immediate spirit dimension that you find yourself in straight after death, and you drift up to more rarefied dimensions that are angelic, in which there are spirit entities, higher beings, into dimensions of greater spiritual evolution. The process is the same for you and me on Earth.

Some people are very set inside their personalities, their religions, their lives. They know what they know. They are often very set into the place where they live. And perhaps they haven't moved very far at all throughout the whole of their life. They are in a cosmic play called the mundane life of Joe Smith, pig farmer. But as you ponder your life, and you meditate and discipline yourself, you become more and more open and infinite.

Then, as you travel around the world, you will soon see that nothing is absolute. Everything is fluid and shifting, and then you become less and less dogmatic about what *this* evolution means. You become less and less certain that the world and the perceptions of Joe Smith, a pig farmer from Little Rock, Arkansas, is what you are.

You begin to see that you are multifaceted, global, and that you exist in a cosmic place. You can live anywhere and adapt to anything; you can embrace many ideas and philosophies. You soon see that you are truly universal and that you are not limited necessarily to the planet Earth, but that you can extend your mind beyond it. Eventually, you'll see that you are a multidimensional being who is straddled across all eternity. You are finite and infinite here and not here simultaneously.

In the process of enlightenment and spiritual growth, you become more diffused. You have probably noticed as your options multiply enormously, you are more at ease with life. By that I mean, you are more detached from the emotions of life and from the tribal mind of your people. You are beyond it all in a way and yet still here.

The same process, I believe, happens to the departed in the spirit worlds. It is the process of melting one's ego, one's perceptions, letting go of old patterns to become a new identity. What you believe a death is what you will see over there. And so people who are very solidly concreted into a particular mindset would enter, as I said, a spirit dimension of that mindset. There, they would no doubt bump into other people's spirits that had the same mindset, and everyone could convince themselves that they were the only ones. Like there are a lot of people who think that humans are the only living beings in the universe—an idea that will eventually be proved wrong, no doubt.

But once the spirit has done enough time in a lowly spirit world, perhaps the process takes place maybe impelled by boredom, whereby the spirit decides to travel on to higher ground, and sooner or later he or she finds that there are truly many mansions in my father's house, as Jesus said. Through transcendence, your identity melts, but it doesn't disappear.

You start as say, Joe Smith on Earth, and then you become Joe Smith and the first of the spirit world straight after death. And then you're Joe Smith imbued with a new perception and the light of God. And then Joe detaches from his dogma and lets go of his personality, his identity, and he moves up and his personality melts somewhat. So rather than being Joe Smith with a little bit of God force within him as before, he now becomes the God force with a little bit of Joe Smith. It is a slightly different emphasis, isn't it?

On the one hand, you are a personality with a bit of God force swishing around inside of you. And on the other hand, you have melted your personality into the divine light so now you are the God force with a bit of a human identity in it—like you are the God force Joe Smith shaped, say, and the emphasis is different.

If you see what I mean, I can feel this process has been happening in my life. And now I feel only remotely connected to the emotions of life on Earth. I only have a passing interest in the mundane aspects of life. That is very different from where I was, say twenty years ago. I am sure if you have been on the path for any length of time, you would have experienced the same shift.

In talking about spirit worlds, I should mention automatic writing. Automatic writing is a way of connecting to the subconscious. It is fun. You sit in a relaxed state with a pen, and you let your subconscious mind take over. Soon your hand is flying along writing all sorts of stuff that you didn't know you knew.

Some have claimed automatic writing is spirit communication, but I have never been totally convinced that that is necessarily so, but it is a stream of consciousness coming from within you. Automatic writing is often chock-full of relevant stuff. So it has worth. Sometimes that flow of information seems to take on a personality, and people will claim that they are channeling a higher spirit. Again, that channeling may be very possible, but then it's also highly conceivable that all or some of what is being written comes from deep within the mind.

Once you connect with the subconscious inner you, you will find it really does often feel like a totally different person separate from you. Sometimes astral entities managed to communicate via mediums and the entities often assume some special characteristic like they are a Mayan priestess from 600 years ago. The entities are drifting around in a vapid world, a lifeless world, so talking to a human full of life force must be quite alluring to such an entity, and they often seem to make it all sound very fantastic and coherent. They know how to suck people in and how to get them to open up and trust them. I know a bit about the astral world as I have had a lot of trans-dimensional experiences over the years.

I would hover over my in-trance body and perform a few nippy etheric turns. I would see or become aware of astral entities, earthbound spirits or thought forms that look like spirits, but that are really phantoms constructed from thought or astral energy of some kind.

From time to time those astral entities would communicate, and dialogue from them would go off in my mind. I would answer back and interact, and I came to realize that, first, the astral entities can't see you any more than you can see them necessarily. And second, they are just stuck there in the astral, drifting around looking for life force to sustain themselves with. They will tell you things that sound good, like you have been chosen to bring the world the great secrets of the cosmos and that you are being granted great powers and that all will be revealed at a later date, blah, blah, blah.

It all sounds very grandiose, and it may convince the gullible, but such practice is shot full of holes if you look at it with a bit of skepticism. If you ever come across one of those entities or if a character appears to you through automatic writing or through the Ouija board and you find yourself communicating with an entity that claims great things, the way to handle it is this: Ask it questions that will back it into a corner. Ask it to describe its world. And when it says it knows everything, ask it something technical, like how big is the Planck length? The correct answer is 1.6 times 10 to the power of minus 35 of a centimeter. If it can't answer technical stuff that any bright thirteen-year-old physics student could answer, then you at least know where you stand.

Shamanism

Shamanism is very valid as a means of communication using the energy or spirit of nature—the nature self as I like to call it. There is great teaching in nature, and the current vogue for the medicine woman or the shaman has reentered our consciousness as people seek to discover their natural self and the simple wisdoms of the past.

A shaman's teachings don't usually offend against any religious or spiritual ideals. Many people, especially in America, have gone back to the ways of the Native people returning to the spiritual simplicity we have lost in the hubbub of modern life and materialism.

If you are drawn to shamanism, I will certainly encourage you because the more that you can align to the nature self, the more purity and clarity you will develop within you.

How to Enter Mysterious Worlds

I now offer you a way to enter into those mysterious worlds that I have been discussing where higher beings dwell.

In Greece in ancient times the Delphic Oracle, a medium if you are like, sat in a cave on a tripod thrown over a big bowl made of metal filled with water to form a large mirror. She entranced herself and looking into the mirror made pronouncements. Some were of a personal nature for the people present, and some were political or military decrees like who would win the Trojan Wars and stuff like that.

The cave and the bowl apparatus were called a psychomanteum. You can build your own psychomanteum in your house. I have one at my place in a small closet.

Action Step: You need two mirrors. Place them on the floor standing up straight and facing each other about a yard apart. Put them somewhere quiet such as under the stairs or in a closet. You will need privacy. And you will need about enough space for yourself as well. But you need to be somewhere quiet and in semi-darkness.

Place the two mirrors facing each other so that they reflect back and forth off each other. Next, put a candle on the floor in the center of one of the mirrors. Once you have tinkered with the mirrors for a bit to get the angle right, the light of the candle knocks back and forth off each mirror and sets up an infinite reflection that goes down the center of each mirror. It is a pathway.

How many times you see the candle reflected in the mirrors will depend on the angle of the mirrors and how big they are. But you should be able to see the candle reflected ten to fifteen times. The candle forms a roadway or a tunnel going off into the distance. It's most eerie and rather beautiful in a way. I always burn incense. But if the spot you have chosen is very stuffy, then you might not. Now sit to the side of one mirror and try not to get your reflection in the mirrors as you don't want to interrupt the tongue of light that is reflected up the center.

If you have a metronome or some soft meditation music that you normally play, then use that to enter into a meditative state. But don't close your eyes. Stare down the center of the mirror and follow the tunnel inward. From time to time pull the tunnel back toward you with your feelings so your consciousness goes down the tunnel and pulls back from the tunnel, alternating.

After a while the center of the mirrors may appear to wobble and go milky or hazy. If so, you will get the impression you see faces there and often you will. Bit by bit those faces come out of their spirit world down the tunnel, and you will see them most clearly. It's best not to try this when you are feeling negative or if you are drinking alcohol or on drugs or if you are into any of the black arts because what may come out of the mirrors might give you a bit of a nasty turn.

As a researcher and a seeker of information, I have given it a go and this setup worked well. Though it's a bit eerie, it's still quite beautiful. I have never come across anything that is real negative or scary. Spirits are like mist; they can't really hurt you.

The psychomanteum might take a bit of time to get going. You should always protect yourself before you start with a simple prayer, and you should be patient. You may find that the first time you try the exercise you will just have a sensation of something being there, but you will not see anything. Yet if you go into your psychomanteum time and again, the tunnel to the other worlds opens up more and more and you will see things brilliantly, really. The psychomanteum teaches you things. It's part of the great journey of life.

9

The Auditory and Visual Sixth Sense:
The Subtle Energy of Clairvoyance

Your subconscious mind has to establish a vocabulary, a language of pictures and symbols, motifs of the mind that you can understand like it's teaching you a new language.

The inner voice is not particularly accurate about making predictions about the future, but it can give you perceptions of current energy that will assist you to make very accurate predictions about what may happen in the short term. That is the auditory sixth sense. I am talking about words or sounds going off in your head, words that contain information. The information might be from your psychic faculty and tell you about a person that you are with, or it may be more of an inner knowing, where the voice within is talking about situations.

Whatever the nature of the clairvoyant inner voice, if you develop it accurately, it will be very useful to you. The problem lies with the quality of the information you receive. For normally the voice you hear in your head is, of course, your own. Often it's giving you ideas, opinions, and information that are not extrasensory or psychic—and often not even correct conjecture and speculation. The problem is to first bring the clairvoyant auditory energy forward to develop it so that you *do* get information in this way. And then you have to be able to *differentiate* between it, the ESP, and what is normally going off in your head.

The other technical problem we face is that of schizophrenia; even a mild form of the disease triggers voices in the head. So if a person suffers from a mental condition, it's easy for him think it's the sixth sense or spirits or whatever, rather than accepting that it is generated internally via a fault in the brain mind mechanism.

The other possibility that most mental health practitioners wouldn't encompass, but one that I believe is probably true, is that there are some people whose etheric is damaged or flapping loose. I have seen alcoholic street people who have a chakra hanging off and their etheric is like a torn curtain. People like these aren't protected on an etheric energy level, so they start to trip across back and forth in and out of this world and into the astral world.

The wino may not necessarily be schizoid, but being unprotected as they are, I believe they are actually hearing the mental telepathic voices of astral entities. Extremes of drugs and alcohol rip the etheric to shreds and leave you vulnerable. Once the life force is damaged and when it is not booming out, because one is dominated by negative mental thoughts or one is at a low inverted state of energy obsessed with life and its problems, then the protection, the barrier that the etheric sets up, begins to deteriorate, and one may become aware or fall prey to astral entities. Those entities, of course, are in a dimension that permeates ours so they are close at hand. However, lest you should worry, don't. One's energy has to fall a very, very long way before this kind of thing happens.

Then there is another example of extrasensory auditory experiences that are sounds that are not of this world. They are not words going off in your head, but they appear to be outside of you. External, extrasensory sounds like you hear a voice out of nowhere, and you are alone maybe out in nature with no one around. The great Scottish medium Daniel Hume, who lived in the mid-1880s, was out in a garden one day, and he heard a voice near him calling, "Over here, over here." He heard the voice several times but could see nothing near him. He walked over in the direction of the sound, and as he did so, the limb of a large tree that he had been standing under fell and crashed upon the very spot he had been on, not a moment before. The voice saved his life.

At the seminars I used to give in the mountains of New Mexico, people reported hearing singing. The seminars were held in a forest at 11,000 feet up in the mountains, miles from anywhere. We had about sixty people in each weeklong event, and in each seminar about twenty to twenty-five of the participants would report hearing the strange singing sounds. Some heard female voices, some heard male voices, Altos, tenors, and some reported both. I did twelve sessions over the years. And the singing was reported every time.

I would reckon about 200 or so people heard it over the years. I heard the female voices about half a dozen times and the altos once. The Mist, as we called the seminar event, was a kind of doorway that opened up to show the participants the presence of other spiritual worlds. I would give the people etheric exercises, and we would set up a process around the etheric bubble meditation—the same one I introduced to you earlier in this book. The process created a tunnel much like the psychomanteum, also discussed earlier—a tunnel of energy that traverses the astral worlds and went into the celestial worlds. From there, sounds and music would flip across into our world, which, in this case, was a mountaintop in New Mexico in the Sangre de Cristo range.

I have also heard music harps and acoustic instruments and some sounds that are completely out of this world that can only be described as similar to lutes and other medieval instruments. Voices and extrasensory sounds that are or that appear to be external to you are rare. But they are quite amazing when they happen, and they should be noticed and made special.

The internal extrasensory voice is the one that we concentrate on, as that is where the real benefits lie. The problem is getting your normal mental voice out of the way so that you can differentiate between it and your extrasensory voice, quietening the internal dialogue that Carlos Castaneda called stopping the world.

This technique is not a five-minute task, and it's pointless my telling you that it is. It takes discipline and time and tenacity. It comes from mental control and the ability to entrance your mind while staying awake. But presuming that you would like to come along the journey with me, here is how you go about developing it, or how you polish it up, if you already have that type of mental control and ESP faculty.

To make the faculty almost completely error-free, you have to clear out the mind, uncluttering it. You have to dominate it with your will, and eventually you have to flip it. I will explain each of these processes in turn. Clearing out the mind is settling it. It's processing yourself through the personality's issues and establishing the pathway, the dialogue between your waking state, your intellect, your waking conscious mind, and your inner self, the subconscious self, the inner mind, if you like. That comes about in the way that I have discussed by establishing the two-way dialogue, first in dream recall, and eventually in meditation by the trance state, when you are operating, in effect, in the technology of the super mind, the infinite mind.

Part of the process of quietening comes in the noticing that I spoke of before, as you begin to see life as an external symbol of your subconscious. Once the day-to-day dialogue between you and the subconscious is established, then the subconscious talks to you and tells you about all of the things it has never been able to discuss with you before. It releases energy from its memory banks, so to speak. And it asks you to look at many different symbols, images, ideas, and repressed feelings. Sometimes they are denied reactions and the psychological elements that lie within you.

To do this, your subconscious mind has to establish a vocabulary, a language of pictures and symbols, motifs of the mind that you can understand like it's teaching you a new language. Once that's going okay, the subconscious can have a jolly good chat with you. And that chat may take a few years as usually it will have quite a few issues to get off its little chest. As that dialogue happens, you begin to learn a lot about yourself and the hidden nature of your subconscious memory.

Now those thoughts and feelings and memories contained therein may have laid there as a dead weight for a long time. They are released by you, and as they are released by you, the subconscious mind lightens up and becomes more opaque. Its issues are resolved and healed and stacked in little files marked over and over and your energy takes on a more powerful comprehensive alignment. Much of the subconscious's repressed energy is given off, released to disappear forever.

In the watching and listening and comprehending of the subconscious, it becomes brighter and lighter and less trouble and less psychologically dumpy. (I am not sure if one can refer to one's psychology as dumpy, but I am sure you know what I mean.) It's the process of lightening up deep within in a place that you do not normally access, attending to the inner demons and releasing them, and seeing that they aren't really demons and that they are only causing you trouble because you haven't listened. Once you do listen, they become white swans and they fly away to other lands, gone forever.

The subconscious processing is ongoing, but there comes a time when enough of the process has completed, and you are very clear, crystal clear, on an inner level, and now you can sit in silence in a meditation state and your subconscious isn't uncomfortable with the experience of feeling the need to express itself via words going off in your head.

Normally, as soon as you pause mentally from the activity of your life or you quiet the mind like in sleep, for example, then the subconscious, seeing an opportunity to get a word in edgeways, starts up either talking to you directly in dreams, or if you are awake, it triggers thoughts in the waking mind hoping to draw your attention to its needs.

It's much like having a prisoner in your attic who has been trapped there for decades. Whenever the house goes quiet, the prisoner cries out for help. But once you have talked to the prisoner, and you have taken time to notice it, and you have tended to the prisoner's needs, and you have sorted out its issues and told the subconscious it can't leave the house as you are still alive in the human body, but that you will make every effort to make it stay as comfortable as possible, then it goes quiet. And after that the subconscious only chirps up when you see something you haven't seen. Gradually you dream less but you experience bigger and better visions.

Setting the subconscious is part of the process while simultaneously you have to settle the waking intellect, for there is no point in having the subconscious quiet if the intellect is jabbering away. How will you do that? Slowly, that's how, I am afraid.

You will begin to push the intellect's free rein, especially when it comes to drifting through endless thoughts in an unfocused way. You have to teach it to focus. Then you have to teach it silence. It's almost impossible to silence the intellectual inner dialogue right away, as it has ruled the roost for many years. It has no need to learn any new ways, and you have never shown it those ways or asked it to act any differently.

First and foremost, the process is one of exercising your will and pushing against the intellect, against the waking mind. Every time the mind worries, remember to say, *I will handle that later.* Or say, *I don't accept that negative energy. I am light and peace and I operate in a totally positive mode.* Say, *All is well,* and so on.

Push, push, push and don't let it regress and get away with things, especially when you are tired or a bit low. Of course, you will help your cause a lot if you can learn to discipline your life even a little. Discipline quietens the mind, as does fasting.

Action Step: Try this. Get a candle and sit by it quietly in semi-darkness with a stopwatch. Blank your mind and see how long you can still the mind before any mental word comes forward. Don't worry for now about trying to rid yourself of mental images the mind may want to think about or mental pictures it might offer you. Dismiss those and try to get into control of just the talking.

Sit, blank your mind, start the watch, and see how long you can go before a word comes into your mind. Make a note of each of your times in your famous little notebook, which by now is ram-jam full of stuff. Keep your batting scores, your times, so you can look at them at a later date.

You may find that you can do this candle process quite well, right off. Usually anything over five seconds without a word coming forward in your mind will be fairly good for starters, and over ten seconds is very good. And if you can do thirty seconds or more without a word coming forward from your inner mind, you probably don't need this candle exercise at all.

Practice the candle/stopwatch exercise for a while, and you will be amazed how quickly the mind learns to back off. But it is only in the silent gaps that you can properly access your auditory ESP, that you can know, really know, that those words appearing in your head are not just your ordinary mental faculty jabbering away to you.

Your auditory ESP is almost never wrong, while your mental dialogue may be wrong or right or somewhere in between. Therefore, it's vital for you to know which is which. It's in the gap or silence of the mind that you are able to differentiate. It's not a perfect science, but it's fairly decent. You get good at the practice over the years.

Once you stop the mind giving you endless words, you can then hook in a symbol or an action, much like the three fingers together that I spoke of earlier. That hook acts as your biofeedback mechanism for the order that comes from your will that says, *Close off the mental dialogue now, this second, for the next fifteen to twenty seconds.* Your closed-down mechanism could be a word you use like *shush* or *shushudishush*, which is one that I have used. Or it could be something that you program into the mind like you click your fingers twice next to your ear when you want mental silence. Eventually the mechanism could just be one almost silent click that you could do even with your hand by your side where you could set up a biofeedback mechanism by just *thinking* about clicking your fingers.

Do you remember that song from the dance routine in *West Side Story* where the dancers were clicking their fingers while singing, "When you're a jet"? You could just recall that scene or anything that you prefer that fits well for you, anything that will work as your personal symbol or mechanism for the clicks. The point is you want to be able to close down the mind instantly at any time, in any circumstances, not just in meditations.

You may be walking along and you will do the click in some way. Or you put your three fingers together and activate the sixth-sense faculty. By these two simple actions you told the brain, the intellect, *Go down to a slower brain speed please and remain mentally silent for as long as possible.*

As you get used to this paused moment of control, you will ask the higher power within you for an instant perception, a readout like, *Is this market in pork bellies going up or down or sideways in the next hour or what?* In the blank space, the inner knowing, your ESP gives you the answer through the auditory faculty. Or your question maybe about a person you are with right now. So you quietly click, click, or you just think about click-clicking and you ask your question relating to that indi-vidual. Remember, it's hard for your auditory ESP to see far into the future. It can't do that very accurately. But it's excellent about telling you about what is here and now in front of you this moment.

Another aspect of auditory clairvoyance is the fact that you have to eventually flip your mind around. Let me give you the concept in principle so you will be able to work it out for yourself, given time. The inner dialogue that we all possess is all pondering and won-dering and confusion and speculation. Too much of the dialogue is full of negative waves and doubts and uncertainties and a lack of self-image and a host of other negative sentiments.

It's very rare that a person has a naturally posi-tive inner dialogue. Many people have developed over the years, through training, a totally positive external self—meaning that they don't voice negative sentiments. Their attitude, their external attitude is totally positive, as far as the outside world is concerned.

But flipping the inner voice takes a bit more effort. It's done by pushing constantly against the negative over a period of time until you control your inner dialogue to such an extent that the positive energy within you takes on a critical mass—that is, it makes up more than half of your total memory, your psychology. Eventually, when that happens, a pole shift suddenly takes place inside of you. All of an instant, your inner voice goes on from partially or totally negative to 100 percent totally positive all the time. Often it even countermands the intellect, which I find cute.

Your intellect, then, may have doubts over an issue, but the inner voice knows and it says it will be fine, go ahead or when it needs to instruct you of a possible difficulty or uncertainty, it doesn't operate with negative dialogue or dire warnings and worry and so on. It comes at you equitably saying in a positive way something like, *See this person here, Ducky, the one that you are talking to right now, here in this alley behind the grocery store? This person has an energy level less than 1. Please notice and accept this timely information. And please vote with your feet like lickety split, Ducky, like, right now would be best.*

I can't say I know when the mental pole shift might take place for you; perhaps it already has. But the idea is to get the process going so that you are reaching for it, developing critical mass, and heading for a place or dimension of love and positive ways.

If you can make even part of the journey right now, it will make an enormous difference to you, for as the mental pole shift approaches, there comes in energy, and with that energy comes even more perception and a heightened sixth sense of all kinds, but especially of the auditory kind. For in the negative, in the worry of life, you climb up the etheric, but there is also a technological etheric aspect to this in that, through negative energy, you set up imploding waves in the etheric that are falling in on you, curving back toward you. And also, emotion creates rolling waves of energy that ripple through the etheric, moving waves of energy that are usually going downward, for the most part anyway.

Those emotional waves carry energy away from the crown chakra and away from the heart. That is why you lose your compassion and sense of love when suffering negative emotion. The rolling waves also burn up and waste energy imploding and folding and tumbling as they do. That is why worry and emotion tire you out, and the waves rolling downward toward the ground don't help you as they pull energy away from the seat of your perception and power—the inner knowing center in your subtle body, the crown chakra.

That's partly why it's hard to perceive and to get yourself sorted out when you are in an emotional upset. The power of perception, the energy of your life, is flowing the other way toward your feet. At the very moment when you are upset and you need to have all your guns blazing on an energy level, you are actually doing the opposite by carrying yourself down to a slow oscillation as your etheric flows with its wave-like downwardness establishing rolling energy that travels through the etheric toward the lower chakras and into the ground at your feet.

To summarize, the auditory sixth sense is very handy, yet it poses problems in separating it from your regular inner dialogue. You have to accommodate the subconscious by getting in touch with it. And you have to train the intellect to shut up and sit down. You have to police your words and become totally positive. Eventually you have to police your silent dialogue to do the same so it gets critical mass and flips over to the positive side. To make the auditory sixth sense work well for you, you need those precious seconds of mental serenity, complete mental silence, a defined gap in the eternal silence. You need that silent moment so you can correctly engage your auditory faculty of all knowing.

The Visionary Sixth Sense

I have told you before about the sensuality of feelings in the sixth sense. Now I have had a chance to lay out the correct approach to the auditory sixth sense. Let us now talk about the visionary sixth sense and discuss how you are sidled up to that. Of course, it goes almost without saying that through dream analysis, you are setting up the visionary process in motion. Yet again, you are telling the power that is within you that visions and dreams and symbols are important to you.

The next thing that is vital is your ability to meditate and entrance your mind. If you are a novice at meditating, then get yourself a theta metronome. It sounds a sequence of beeps oscillating at 4 to 6 cycles a second. Hearing that, the brain starts to slow down to the same deep oscillation automatically. If you meditate regularly, you will begin to see things in the mind's eye appearing in your sight even though you have your eyes closed.

I explain this process in more depth in my book, *Whispering Winds of Change.* Here are the main points:

When you first start meditating, you will see colors crossing your eyes. They're from the optic nerve. It's a bit like when you look at the sun and then shut your eyes quickly. Then you see a golden blob of light, the residue of photons that have impacted your retina.

After the colored blobs come and go, you will see symbols crossing from left to right or right to left in arced trajectories, those symbols will be on a dark background and may be strung together in sequences. You may see trees for two weeks, for example, and houses for a week and then animals and then geometric shapes. These symbols are from your subconscious mind. They may not mean very much at first; it's just a way of the subconscious releasing energy. Sometimes it's the subconscious mind setting up references, language if you like.

If you see a human eye close up, it's a subconscious way of saying *I* like in me, like you and me, our self, combined as an entity. The symbols appear in arced trajectories because your eyes are curved. After these come and go, you return to looking at just the darkness for a while and then you may begin to see symbols or even whole pictures or scenes coming up the center of your vision. Remember when I say the center of your vision, I mean the center of the visual screen you have with your eyes closed. Those symbols may be in a dark light, but not as dark as the subconscious strings of symbols from before, or they may be surrounded by vivid bright light, lively and full of life, surreal in its beauty.

These up-the-middle symbols or pictures come, I believe, from elsewhere deep within beyond the subconscious—through it, let's say, from some greater consciousness such as the global mind, the collective unconscious, or even the God force beyond. They are clear and bright and they move at incredible speed.

I started seeing letters of the alphabet often lit in gold moving at extremes of velocity toward me. You don't have time to engage your thinking to watch them. You have to allow the symbol or picture to impact the retina. Then you review it from the memory that that event creates in the same way, as I discussed remembering cards when counting at blackjack.

To me, the letters became words over time and eventually sentences and finally whole paragraphs. I think that my ability has gone up over the years. For while the speed of the symbols was initially very quick, too quick for me as often as not, in recent times, I have found much more time to view what's coming up the pike. And now it's moving at a more manageable pace. I can now read about half a page of text at one glimpse. Simultaneously with fast moving symbols up the center, you might see pictures, scenes, like seeing a living snapshot of things happening elsewhere.

The whole picture is the symbol, like the one I told you about when I saw the castle covered in seaweed come up out of the lake.

How you get to this visionary sixth sense is you have to teach yourself to let go and to descend deeper and deeper into a delta brain wave state, which would be

1 to 3 cycles per second, and you have to train yourself to stay awake. It comes with training and practice. The technique is not that hard. I have known loads of people who can do it quite well, even after a few tries and very well after several months of daily practice.

Life is a trade-off; you have to put in to get stuff out. In that deep brain state, visions come. Sometimes you look and see people elsewhere on Earth doing mundane things; more often than not, sometimes you may be looking up the near-death tube and see dimensions or spirits. Some of those aren't too flash, but you get to see them anyway. Some of the dimensions you see are brilliant and celestial and the God force is there. It's all the love you have ever seen or felt or ever hoped to be a part of.

Sometimes, if the vision comes from another world, and it's not a part of your subconscious or your intellect, it can describe future events—predictions like those of Nostradamus, for example. I have seen visions of the Chinese army marching—that was very disturbing—and other visions of parts of Europe in trouble and events that will take place much later on. I have seen visions of a technical nature that have given me a lead or clue with some of the experiments I have tried. I have seen visions that deal with my family and its well-being. Last but not least, I have had a bunch of visions that helped me to understand the etheric.

In the vision process, I see the vision and then I enter a description of what I saw on my computer file. That's my notebook. I go back to it and try to unravel what it means at a later date, much like the dream recall exercise. Some visions are accompanied by a very distinct feeling.

The symbol or picture automatically tells its own story.

It's the technical ones I have most difficulty with, the ones that deal with dimensions of space time. They are the hardest to figure out. But the universe at large is always there to help us, and the more times or not, when I am very stuck, I will pull the answer to me in some way. One example: I was in the local bookshop and I opened to a page in a book that described all the stuff I had thought of. Recently, I saw a vision that explained an aspect of space time symmetry. I was stuck as I didn't know the concept well enough, let alone comprehend even the basic mathematics of it. Here's how the answer came to me: I picked up a load of books at the store. Among one of the books was one that I thought dealt with genetics such as DNA. It turned out that I got the wrong book. Although I was initially disappointed with myself for not watching carefully, when I opened the book, I wound up with all that I ever needed to know about symmetry and the great unified theory and a host of other stuff that was most handy and very explanatory.

Action Step: Lie north to south and open up via the bubble technique, and then try raising yourself up slightly over your body so that you are now hovering over your body, say eighteen inches above it. Then spin yourself around so that your etheric head is where your feet would normally be. Then breathe in and mentally blow yourself up like a balloon and let out the air and come back to your normal size and don't fall asleep.

Try to stand upright and walk out of your body and out through the wall of the bedroom, or wherever you are. It's unlikely that we will actually get out of the body at this point, but the action creates looseness and pliability and opens you up. Next, pause for a moment and then come back to the mental picture of hovering over yourself again at eighteen inches above your body.

Do the head-to-toe visualization once more and breathe deeply. Then trance yourself deeper and deeper. By now you should be very light and airy and hovering slightly out of the body as you hover in that open, in between state. Watch what comes to your mind's eye. If nothing comes right away, wait. Watch and notice if your subtle feelings are showing you things. See if you can get the impression of other beings in the room. Perhaps you will see the end of the near-death tube especially if you are relaxed enough and far enough down the brain oscillation scale.

If you don't see the end of the tube, you may find that you are off to the right of it or to the left of it, slightly skewed at an angle. This is because there is a singularity of energy at the mouth of the tube, at its entrance. And that singularity pushes you off a little way. It can take you a while to get around to the front of the tube where you can look up it. But patience is a virtue. It's vitally necessary when you are playing around looking at other worlds and practicing so you can look at stuff that no one normally looks at.

When you finish this floating exercise as described, write down anything that happened and make sure you close yourself down by returning the little bubble to the base of the spine, the root, and closing the chakras or set the crown, which never closes.

I'll leave you with this bit of advice: Don't drive your car right after you perform this exercise as you might be a bit disoriented. I went to return my car to my garage straight after one of these sessions and nearly flattened a pedestrian whom I didn't see, and she would have been up the near-death tube herself—quite quickly I would imagine—if I had not heard the banging on the trunk of my car with a hand and if she hadn't been good at jumping.

10

The Subtle Energy
of Relationships

*Relationships are really a school you attend in which
what you are is reflected back toward you; it's a mirror.*

Following on from the last chapter's discussion of the
subtle energy of clairvoyance, I am applying that energy
in relationships and discussing how that relates to the
masculine and feminine within. There is an extrasensory perception has to how energy flows back and forth
between us all, and we can also look at the deeper psychological and metaphysical aspects that impact the
way men and women are sometimes powerful, others
less powerful.

How you gather power is by being in control of the
energy that you do have. Most people don't really understand that. They think they need to have an external

worldly power that exerts influence over others. In fact, the more people you have to influence and be responsible for in life, the more you encumber yourself with things you have to do; you lose sight of self in the sacred journey.

Having great power over people can be a tremendous burden and misfortune rather than being a good thing, for having power over others kids the ego of its godlike powers. And that's an illusion. It only serves to make the ego stronger and harder to deal with in the end. Dealing with people can burn you out, take you into the world of emotion and ego where you would be better off in the world of serenity and the God force. Dealing with people often forces you into struggle and away from the sixth sense and flow. There is a secret to free flow. It's the idea that the universe at large, nature, your energy mix with the God force within you will bring you everything that you need.

Things come effortlessly in the fullness of time. The more people you are involved with, the more mind games you have to deal with. Once you question if one is too involved with people, have you allowed yourself to be sucked in? Is there any space for the real you? The inner you? Also question if that involvement that you have with people is infringing upon them, and changing their perspective. It's a powerful person who can walk through life and leave things as they are, even when he or she can perceive that by leaving things as they are, the situation might get more imbalanced.

The purpose of life, in my view, is to move through it effortlessly, consuming as little as possible, touching as little as possible, perceiving, watching, learning without really changing too much, except those people who asked to be changed. If in life, you have to push and pull and strive and fight with people, you have to ask yourself, *Am I following the parabolas of energy that are the most positive for me? That have the most energy for me?* You need to engage the subtlety of your feelings in the sixth sense to discover whether or not you are trying to put a square peg into a round hole.

Looking toward the beauty and flow of things, you will soon see the natural way. In any given situation, there is the path of least resistance. It's the path on which you don't have to fight to get what you want. You don't have to terrorize, manipulate, maneuver, control, or regulate. What you need, in my view, is inner power, personal charisma, a spiritual power, an extrasensory perception that makes you bigger than life—a silent power that says you are beyond the mundane things. How you garner that energy is through compassion, kindness, introspection, and solidity.

The idea is to understand yourself as a spiritual being and evolve quietly and gently through the human experience, developing confidence, projecting out into the world lovingly and with caring and without the need to infringe upon others. It's important for me to remind you about that. I know we talked about it in passing in a previous chapter, but let me go over it here. For it is the key to perception and balance in relationships.

The concept of infringement is misunderstood. Here's the crux of it. The world has a rhythm, a destiny, a karma—in a way it's a collective karma. But we are all inside the one human mind, the global mind. And each of us makes up a molecule of that global mind. We don't have all the answers so we are forced to move along as humans one step at a time.

The global mind and the individual evolutions that make up their global mind are entitled to their own decisions. They are entitled to make the wrong decisions. But there is no right and wrong, really, there's only the infinite love of the God force and the winding journey we all make attempting to return back to our celestial source.

In other words, we have plenty of time to work it all out, and we are entitled to head up the wrong path, entitled to marry the wrong people, entitled to get involved in the wrong deals, eat the wrong foods, and so on. People have to carve out their own destiny; otherwise, they don't learn anything. The philosophy of non-infringement says that everyone is moving along according to the dictates of either their ego personality or their inner infinite self, or a mixture of the two. Where they are going is where they are supposed to be going and what shouldn't be changing that.

Infringement is interference. It is manipulation, control, psychological mind games, emotional blackmail, contractual nastiness, and financial control and terror tactics that deal with money and power. You should be careful to avoid that. Of course, as a part of an evolution we are infringed upon all the time, especially by our governments and our legislators who enforce upon us unreasonable control, often for their own ends rather than our benefit. Unfortunately, we have to accept that as part of our karma and know that one day the system will have to change.

The lessons of our life's journey are complex. We are here to learn to love in a dimensional manipulation and hatred is common. We have to become courageous where there's much fear and insecurity. We have to detach when everyone is trying to suck us in as much as possible. We have to have faith in ourselves, when often people are trying to pull us down. And we have to believe in abundance when people talk of crisis and lack.

It's a funny old game. But the essential lesson is that we are here to learn to go beyond our fears, and to learn to love, to learn to become love, to express love in a dimension that is fearful.

The second lesson is to learn about oneself and one's relationship to others and the creator. Of course, the expression of that creator comes through us as the creative force within us. So creativity is part of our lesson as well. That's why relationships are so important because relationships are really a school you attend in which what you are is reflected back toward you; it's a mirror. That's why people suffer a lot of imbalance, emotion, and difficulty in relationships, because they are looking at themselves, and it makes them uncomfortable, fearful and angry.

The sixth sense is that all knowing lies deep inside, and through it you will know the communication, the love, the fine balance that is needed. You come to the Earth plane, and you incarnate to experience this lifetime. You experience it in the context of being an eternal being positioned inside your body, inside your tribal heritage, inside the society, as a family member, with your partner of choice, and perhaps children. All of these are the placement of the incarnation, so to speak, where you find yourself. Then interacting with others and being in relationships is how you put the experience into action. Extending your perception to relationships not only makes them operate better, but you understand yourself and the true nature of your spiritual journey.

Look at People as Infinite

The first thing to remember is, you have to look at people as infinite. It's easy to say and hard to do. Think about everybody you might have talked to yesterday or anyone you thought of. How many times did you think of them in terms of their being an angel inside a body, infinite? Probably very few times as normally we relate to others in the strictly physical material sense as in Harry as a body, as a male, as a carpenter, a neighbor.

It's rare to think of people as spirits when you sit on a bench in the park, watching people, perhaps running through the exercises I've talked about, trying to see people as angels. See through their physical body and their characteristics, their tribal energy, and see if you can see them an oscillating angelic force field, momentarily trapped inside the mind/body mechanism.

Looking at people in this way, you get a whole new perception of what they are and who they are. You can see the infinity in their eyes, in their expression, and you can see the way energy flows around them at lightning speed.

People are so much more than we know and understand. And you and I are so much more than you and I could ever possibly understand. So turn a soft eye upon your brothers and sisters and see them in the same context as you would see yourself as an infinite being—that is, offer them compassion, hard as that might be sometimes. Understand they are weak, but they are learning as we are all learning. We are learning to become infinite in our perspective of self, and it may take a little while. But in the end, we're all on the winding path back to God. We never left our infinite state. We're still in that infinite dimension of goodness, even though our physical body is here on the Earth plane.

It's hard to think like this at first, especially about others, but try it. Your boss may be the biggest manipulative jerk in the whole world, but he is an infinite jerk. From an energy perspective, if you infringe upon others, you link your karma to that of others; you become responsible for others. You can't go beyond people while you're infringing upon them. And you don't need that kind of impediment. You don't want to be responsible for unnecessarily changing people's lives, and you don't want to hold yourself back.

Let them be and let them go. Even if that causes you pain. It's the right way, the spiritual way. Imagine a situation where someone has decided to go north as that, in their opinion, is where their highest destiny lies. But you knew from your intellect to influence them in some way to go south. All of a sudden, they've met the wrong bloke headed off to the Yucatan, and their whole destiny has changed maybe for the worse.

Maybe it'll take them this whole lifetime to get back to where they were going destiny-wise the day they decided to go north before you stuffed it up for them and sent them south.

Once you've raised your energy and once you've learned to see properly, then you'll stand as an angel, not as a man or woman. You'll stand to one side, helpful to those that ask of your perception, your expertise, and non-infringing with those that don't ask. You gain strength that way, and you prepare your evolution lickety split. I've seen it happen so many times.

If someone comes to you and asks for your opinion, give it to them. They've asked you as part of their karma, their decision, their destiny, and they may or may not act on what you tell them. That's okay. If someone comes to you and asks for your help, do your best to help them. But if they don't ask, do nothing.

Here is something I used to tell the people in my seminars. Try it for yourself. If two people are talking about, say, a car trip, and they're wondering what road to take, and you know the shortest and best and most effective way to get where these people are going, don't tell them. Stand there listening to the discussion and discipline yourself to say nothing. Imagine yourself as a spirit hovering high in the room near the ceiling, just watching. When they pick the road that you know is blocked because the bridge fell into the river last week, let them pick it. Don't say anything. Not unless they specifically turn to you and ask which way to go. Don't tell them what, you know. It's very hard to take this kind of detached position. We're trained to be involved, to interfere; we're trained the other way, aren't we?

Here's another one. Next time your friend is in a clothing shop and picks something that looks absolutely ghastly, say nothing, let them buy it. Now, if they asked you what you think, don't dissuade them entirely, just suggest that they try on a few more items, like maybe another thousand, before finally making up their mind, Try to let people act out their decisions without too much input or influence from you.

The problem with our world is that we all infringe upon each other way too much. And those in authority are almost fascist in the way they seek to control us. They haven't seen extremes of control. If only we'd all back off a bit and we understood non-infringement, we'd have low taxes, safe neighborhoods, and the spirit of love and cooperation in our societies and families. It'll take time. But you can start the process right now, for you understand and know.

As you focus on non-infringement, it becomes your teacher. It will show you things inside other things, and it will show you aspects of compassion and the infinity within, that you may not have seen before. You become bigger once you're no longer involved, once you're no longer infringing. Most suffer from having to manipulate others needing to control them as a power trip or through insecurity. This is seen especially in interpersonal relationships. It's all to do with fear and insecurity. It sets up the pattern, and from that the infringement flows.

In the fear, you stiffen, and so you can bring yourself to let go and allow others their chosen path. The fear stifles us and forces us to hold on too tightly to life, and to circumstances and to relationships. That is why we cling to control. Fear of loss, really, isn't it? In the end, you can't flow down the river of life if you can't become vulnerable and let go, and flow and trust. You can't find yourself as an angel, as an infinite being, if you can't become vulnerable and let go of where you are today. For what you are, what you believe, may have become old and stale, and it might be holding you back. In the end, you have to let it go.

It's odd really. But to discover your highest potential, your highest energy, your sixth sense, you have to agree to let go and lose yourself a bit. Fear kills off relationships, the ego's self-centered and insecure perspective, and its overall survival trip gets in the way of love. Things go wrong. Love is giving people space, letting them be, having compassion for them, and feeling secure without having to imprison others emotionally. But when the ego kicks in, you get scared and insecure and you tend to want to control and that will stifle others and they will react negatively.

You might have been attracted initially to an individual because they were different. Maybe they seemed unusual or interesting, powerful and strong, and then you get into a relationship with them. Each of you enters into the web of the other's energy where you both try to create more power, more energy, and that arrangement usually works initially. Things move faster metaphysically, and you create a quickening. All of that is fine when you're both coming out of love and cooperation, when you're both on your best behavior. But if one or both of you freak out at the speed of things, or you react to the responsibility of the other person in your life, one or both of your egos kick in with its power trip. Things will turn negative. Suddenly one is fearful and wimping out a bit, and perhaps they're trying to hold the other one back.

The stronger one reacts to having energy pulled from them. They want their partner to stay with the pace, and they don't like the implication of what is happening. An energy war develops and goes like this: *It's your turn to do the washing up. I'm tired. I work and pay for this and pay for that and all you do is sit on the couch and watch TV. It's your turn to—whatever.*

So the whole relationship descends into a quagmire. One partner trying to enforce the law, stifling the other standing over them, and the weaker one trying to hold things back controlling and manipulating, cajoling and screaming and shouting to get things to go at their desired pace. Then the situation might change and the gung ho one now has got the flu and he or she wants to pull back. And the slower one is happy and they take control and drive the bus, so to speak, and the gung ho one sooner or later reacts and the war's on again—a teeter totter back and forth.

The other thing that happens in relationships is that often both of you cede a certain amount of your newfound extra power to the other person. But the ego doesn't like to admit that so psychological turf wars ensue where one claims all the power as his, and the other one knows it isn't. It's a political thing that develops when relationships go into tight ego mode, rather than love open mode; a negative polarity shift takes place, and those shifts should be sorted out quickly through love and compassion and good communication.

Quality talking takes place where you and your partner express your concerns, and where you release whatever aggravation has built up and you both listen to the other person and you get a chance to see what's needed. You get a chance to engage your sixth sense to feel how things can best be put back on track, in other words.

Bring your perception of sixth sense to your relationships by watching the flow of energy and reacting with positive action when needed, and not reacting with negative emotion or negative dialogue when you feel uncomfortable. By seeing it all as energy, by watching those reserves of energy ebb and flow, the energy of your family, the home, the energy of each of you—you'll soon see what you need. You can scotch any trouble before it starts and before resentment sets in.

Just ask of your mind, ask it to read the energy of the situation and tell you what's needed. In this way, you become the custodian of the energy of the relationship, and you make adjustments and everything rests in harmony.

Now the way to develop a sixth-sense sensitivity to the energy of your family, your partner, and friends is to ask yourself the standard questions in relation to people's actions. You are looking to use the sixth sense to discover what people's deep inner feelings are in relation to any given action. You engage your perception to delve telepathically into what the subtle message or energy is that underlies that action.

Actions are the external manifestations of thoughts and ideas, and the impulse for those thoughts are always some deep inner feeling. Therefore, action is the external manifestation of a feeling or need or desire. When people act in a certain way, there is an explanation. It may not be obvious to your intellect at first, but to your inner self, to your subtle perception, it's easy to see. By unraveling people's innermost feelings, their actions become obvious.

At any given moment each has an inner message that they're operating under the influence of. It's a beacon they emit. When people talk, there's a message inside the talking isn't there? A message inside their silence when they're not talking. There's always an unfinished agenda. People do not speak from all that they think and feel. They only announce a percentage of their overall reality. That's because they may be covert, but more often than not, it's because they simply are not aware of their subliminal subconscious impulses. They don't know necessarily what is moving them. It may be some very distant feeling in their subconscious of which they are not aware.

You can, however, quite easily discover people's hidden message. Here's a simple way to get you started.

Action Step: Blank your mind. Establish the silent gap we talked about. As the person talks to you, pull them into your concentration. Imagine your etheric arm outstretched. Now you've got an etheric hand at the back of their neck, and you're pulling the person ever so gently toward you, placing them close to you metaphysically and on an energy level.

There's another way of holding people that's a bit more complicated, but easy enough to do. Imagine a beam of light or thin steel rod like a coat hanger wire going from your left eye diagonally across to the other person and imagine the wire or the light going behind the other person's left eye.

So now you're holding them with a beam of light, holding them gently in your visual concentration. You're holding them momentarily with your power, establishing the connection with them just for that instant. There's nothing negative or untoward in holding a person in this way. Concentration is a form of love. When you love someone, you concentrate on them in a positive way; you are there for them, rather than inside your own head, your own thoughts and feelings and needs. Concentration is love, isn't it?

Once you have the other person in your concentration mentally, pull them close to you via the left eye to left eye connection. And by the way, as you do so as you pull them, you may see them tilt ever so slightly toward you.

When you know that you are fully there, completely focus on them. And you're in the blank mind mode, the click-click mode, ask your inner self to finish any uncompleted sentences they may utter. That will give you a guidance as to where they're really at. In effect, you're tapping into their subconscious or tapping into that part of their reality that is unspoken.

Your friend might say, *I would like to go to the movies next Thursday with you, but I'm not sure,* and you blank your mind and ask of your sixth sense to fill in the missing bit. And the answer goes off as words in your head. The first words you hear are always correct. As long as you're in the click-click mode of mental silence, the rest of the sentence comes back to you telepathically from the other person, because your inner self is connected, and it knows. After all, we're all inside the same collective super mind and the same global mind.

Now let's say in this case, the rest of the story in your head through your sixth sense goes like this: *I'd like to go to the movies with you next Thursday, but I'm reluctant because I want to bring my boyfriend. I've noticed subliminally that you look at my boyfriend in a way that seems odd to me, and I feel you might be after him. I don't feel so good about myself. And I also think you're prettier than I am, and better than me and more sexy, and I worry lest you and he hit it off, and I might lose him.*

Generally, the rest of the story or the rest of the sentence that goes off in your head is not usually quite as convoluted as this example I've given, but I've laid it out here in this way so you can comprehend it easily.

Once you've listened to your friend's inner answer, you make adjustments to ease their problems or their issue or their insecurities. In this case, you might talk about how neat her boyfriend is, and you might talk about how happy you are with the boyfriend you've got or in the relationship that you're in, and how you're really committed. You say that people shouldn't infringe upon each other and take each other's boyfriends and girlfriends, and you say all the things that you need to say to reassure your friend that she doesn't have to worry.

You're using your sixth-sense perception to guide her to a safe place so that she's not putting fear in front of your friendship. At this point, it feels safe for her to say, *Okay, I'll come to the movies.* Life is simple when you know what others are really thinking and feeling.

Sometimes when you're in that click-click, mentally blank concentrating mode, asking questions about what others are thinking, you're not necessarily always asking the mind to finish an unfinished sentence. Sometimes you receive or hear from your inner voice information that is adding an extra silent sentence as an explanation that enhances what has already been said.

In this example, you might hear the mind adding a missing bit at the end of your friend's completed sentence. For example, she says, *I don't know if I really want to go to the movies, the weather is bad.* And now you are silent for the rest of it. Her mind comes back to you in a telepathic transfer that says, *I really want to go to the movies, but I want you to drive across town out of your way and pick me up, and by the way, I want you to pay for me as I'm poor and you're well off. Anyway, you always pay for me.* Hearing that telepathically, you can then decide on the basis of the silent information if it's reasonable for you to be the chauffeur and financier of the trip to the movies or not.

Using this telepathic sixth sense, you cut across the unspoken stuff to the real stuff. Try it, you'll find it a lot easier than you think.

It's the same in your business dealings. Often people's agenda in business is one of ego, power, and status, not losing face, positioning and control and so forth. It's not necessarily a money issue all of the time, is it? Sometimes you can offer people status or an ego boost instead of money. So you keep the money and take the humble spot and let the other person have the status and the hoopla.

When you're next at a business meeting, hold each person eye-to-eye, one after the next, as I discussed, and as you hold them, blank your mind and ask inwardly of your sixth sense to tell you what everybody wants. In this way you can cut to the heart of the matter. You can get to the heart of their desires and their needs. And you'll know what's happening next. Everybody wants something. It's not a bad thing necessarily, but it's rare that you meet people who don't want anything, very rare. If you ask constantly of your sixth sense, it will tell you what people want. Even though sometimes their wants are framed inside a hidden emotion, it's still easy for your inner self to work it out, for we're all connected.

Remember, most people have little or no real free will because they don't own their power yet. They only have the potential of free will, the illusion of free will. They don't have a command of the real thing. Therefore, they react to life from a Pavlovian knee-jerk response, moving away from pain, fear, and discomfort, in an effort toward anything that makes for comfort, a cushy life an ego boost, importance, glamour, and status. It's not a bad thing or a good thing; it's just the way we're programmed.

Because of this Pavlovian response, it's easy to figure out people's needs that project the energy of their needs and impulses outwardly, and even though they may hide it in their words, it will be there in the subtle expression. With practice, it becomes simple to understand why people do what they do. Sometimes your inner mind will show you or tell you about the overall feeling or emotion involved, not necessarily the finer aspects of the other person's agenda.

Perhaps the friend that you're asking to the movies doesn't have her agenda formulated yet, and her hesitancy about the trip to the movies lies in an unexpressed or confused feeling deep within her. In other words, maybe on this occasion your friend hasn't got a precise reason why she's reluctant to go to the movies. It is just that other emotions are more important to her right at this moment, like her emotional self is elsewhere.

If the answer to the question you ask of her mind when you're holding her close to you comes back to you a bit scrambled, then go for trying to discover the overall emotion. Just ask your sixth sense, *What is the overall emotion here? What is my friend's overriding feeling at this precise moment?* Simultaneously stretch out an etheric hand and place it on her heart so that you're connected to her emotionally. The sixth sense will translate what it perceives there in the heart chakra, and you'll find out that your friend is not thinking about you or the movies, but in fact, she's worried about a mother who's been a bit unwell lately.

Action Step: Now let's say you have a reason to win somebody over for romantic reasons or perhaps you just like the person and you want to be their friend. First you do the obvious stuff, like putting yourself in the best light possible—take a bath, pitch up on time, looking good, and feeling great. You're ready, you're not plowing into the situation, with one shoe on, one shoe off. You're prepared and you're confident and you're ready.

When you're with that special person, begin to really listen to them, be interested, ask silent questions, and empathize with their inner hidden needs, as well as empathizing with their intellectual self and what they're saying. At the same time, join them on an inner level. Reach out to them etherically, and reach into them and hold their heart in your hand. Imagine you're watching it beating in the palm of your hand. See if, etherically, you can feel its rhythm, its pulse, which can be a very beautiful moment.

As you hold them close in this way, exude love and caring for them. The love transfers instantly, and they feel good and their eyes light up ever so slightly. Watch for that. Often, they're not sure why they suddenly feel so safe and good and relaxed, but they will sooner or later intellectually or subconsciously associate that feel-good factor with you and your presence in their life.

If, for example, you're in very close proximity to the individual in question, like you're dancing with them, see if you can hold their hand or if you can put your finger on their neck. You're trying to find their pulse through the jugular vein or at the wrist. If you can get their pulse, if you can feel it while you're dancing, then go into your click-click blank mode and visualize yourself stepping out of your body etherically. Have your etheric body jump backward into theirs, reverse into their energy, and ask your heart to slow down or to speed up to the rhythm of their heart, which is of course you're listening to by holding their wrist. You join your two hearts together, both beating as one.

It doesn't matter if your heart isn't quite at the same rhythm. It's the etheric entering into the other person's energy and joining them that matters, like your wisdom, inside them, at the same life pulse. It's a way of saying on a cosmic level, *You and I are one.*

You'll be amazed how well this technique works. People really respond to it. You can invent all sorts of techniques and try them out, but always look for the inner way, the inner explanation in life, especially if there's no obvious external intellectual explanation. You have all your normal faculties and a few more besides that are extrasensory, like you really know where everyone's going, and when they'll get there.

My message in this chapter is this: You exercise your spiritual, angelic self through relationship. That's how you discover yourself. That's how you express spiritual action. And it is there that you discover the nature of yourself. It helps you to get shot of the negative bits of self and enhance the positive jolly nice bits.

11

Polarity in the Lightness of Being

A man feels he has power and identity through what he does. A female's identity is more aligned to what she feels.

As you take to a more sacred path and you get a little metaphysics, your perspective changes and you are less a part of a solid world, and more in an opaque world, a translucent world, a world of dimensions and shifting energies. It's a world where you can see through walls, not necessarily with your vision, but with your feelings. A surreal world where the past, present, and outlines of the future coexist, where subtle energies intermingle, shifting and moving, opening some doors for you, and closing others—a surreal world where anything is possible, and the improbable becomes possible.

Sandwiched between the 3-D world and this strange and beautiful opaque world are invisible corridors, passageways that permeate reality, where the spiritual traveler understands the power somewhat, engages the sixth sense, and moves suddenly back and forth through these invisible corridors, here and not here. Now you are a part of a hidden domain, where energy is the currency of choice and a natural humility comes upon you for the God force is more and more present in your life.

Thus we move our perception and commitment from a solid heavy state of evolution to a lighter, more wispy see-through energy state. In that energy state, we begin to perceive the balance necessary to empower our journey, our life, and the whole of nature exists in a tension between polarities. When I say tension, I don't mean stress. I mean it in the sense of electrical or magnetic polarity, like that of a magnet. We see in life, the positive polarity, pushing on the negative and the negative polarity pulling on the positive, That is how energy is created and sustained. It comes from the interaction between opposite polarities.

In your life, your power comes in part from the interaction of your physical strength and your body/mind mechanism, and the life force or God force that is within you. Your energy comes from the interaction of the yin and yang within. So the masculinity within a woman creates a synapse of energy within her femininity, and the femininity in the male interacts with his masculinity. In this way, power is created.

In trying to understand the metaphysical world and its energy, it's important to know that energy that has a positive polarity, yang, tends to move outward, and energy with a negative polarity, yin, tends to move inward. I am not using the words *positive* and *negative* in the sense of good and bad. It's just a way of describing direction. I could easily say that yang is north, and yin is south.

I don't know how you feel about a lot of that yin and yang stuff that you read in books, but much of it puts me to sleep. It's much too wishy-washy. I began to wonder, where is the yin in the female? And where is the yang? And what does it mean anyway? There has to be a technology that applies to this yin and yang stuff that fits into the sixth sense and energy. Sure, you can understand the yin inside the yang, but what does it actually mean to us every day?

Here's the missing bit, the opaque bit in the yin and yang story. It might sound a little different to what you already know, but follow it through, as it will click into place, and you'll see it all in a different light, in the light of the sixth sense.

The **female** has an inner spiritual identity. Think of it as a subtle body, a reservoir of light, a perpetual memory. It makes up her inner spiritual self. That inner spiritual identity is of a positive polarity. It is actually the yang within her. Look at the female's inner traits.

They are spiritual and nurturing. They express love outward, with caring, mothering, compassion, and kindness. They love the Earth and the little things. It is the outgoing supportive energy of femininity.

Yet the physical body of the female is of the opposite polarity, yin, which pulls energy to her. She sucks up the emotions of others, their feelings. She pulls energy and attention to her as she walks down the street. She pulls the baby to her breast. She pulls the male to her body. So her body has the effect of pulling energy in toward her. It is therefore metaphysically an inward energy, and we would therefore consider that it has a negative polarity.

The electricity of the feminine incarnation is created by the tension or synapse between her yang spirituality that is pushing out into life through love and compassion expressing outward and her yin body that is pulling energy inward toward her. A female has to have a balance inside this synapse, between her spirituality and her physicalness. She will have a natural tendency to want to go out and experience the world, to have fun, to interact with others, and she has a need to earn money and wants to have influence and experience life's gifts.

Yet in the meantime, she has to guard her natural spirituality—her softness within. The female is safe and balanced metaphysically because the spiritual energy inside of her, that yang spirituality, pushes out through her etheric, keeping her protected. It has the effect of bouncing away the energy that is coming toward her physical body from the outside world. Her spirituality pushes out on its yang parabola, keeping us safe. That's where her balance lies.

The trick is for her not to become so overworked and stressed, and so much deluded by the mire of the outside world that she goes out on a limb and plops off the edge of her balance into a sea of trouble. A good bit of outgoing energy helps her to earn money, to experience life, to have fun, and to get things done. But if she overdoes it on the outgoing side, her world starts to crack up. She suffers psychological or emotional imbalance, and often her physical body reacts to the loss of velocity and to the loss of her spiritual light. That is why when a female is tired and stressed out, she feels threatened and unable to cope, because what holds her world together metaphysically is the spiritual polarity within her, the positive yang polarity that is pushing out.

Once she overdoes her activity in the external world, if she loses sight of her inner self, then she loses power. It's very subtle, and it's so easy to overdo it and to burn it out. When that happens, the spirituality and the softness are lost, and it can't flow outward properly, and her protection is lost. It's as if her light is cut off and denied an outward expression so it ceases to enliven and to sustain her. It cuts off even from her physical cells. She becomes darker and disconnected from the energy, from the God force.

Now her womanly self, her feminine body, is still sucking energy from all directions. And much of what she pulls to her is not helpful, or it's downright debilitating, so the incoming energy burns her. If the outgoing spiritual light isn't expressing itself strongly, she has no protection metaphysically and the walls of her energy start to crack around her, and she may become insecure and find that she can't hold her life together. This will flatten and rattle her, and survival issues come up. The ego kicks in, outraged by the fact of what she experiences and she may become emotional and upset.

In those reactions, she will burn even more of her reserves of light; she will drain more of her energy and that carries with it the potential of problems or danger. Life may possibly swamp her. She'll be swamped with a tidal wave of incoming energy toward her physical body with little or no protection.

But the female who has agreed to step inside the opaque world of perception inside her sixth sense understands the power. She's not kidded by the mire of the physical world. Glamour is alluring, of course, because it represents power, but it's only in the ego's world. A female with perception has power anyway. She can walk down the tunnels that permeate life, tunnels not unlike those of the psychomanteum discussed earlier.

She can step out of the physical, emotional mind-set of the normal world into another world, another dimension, her mysterious world. Inside that strange and beautiful place she can exercise a special power, moving energy with no effort, commanding her destiny silently and powerfully. She will automatically pull to her all that she wants and needs, and the undesirable energies of life that she is normally subjected to, in the external world, will pass her by, for she will become invisible to them. Or she will just deflect those energies via her shield of spirituality of personal power.

She cannot be inundated by life's energy because she is in control. She is inside her own world, inside a different dimension, living in the physical world, but moving through the silent gaps, the corridors of light, click-clicking as she goes.

When she's in the space between these two worlds, she's behind an invisible wall of violet light. She's behind a solid etheric curtain. In there, she's perpetually safe, she can't be touched, because in a metaphysical sense, she does not exist in the physical plane, She is outside the global mind, deep inside the balance of our spirituality and her yin feminine body, She's finally come home, back to the heartland, back home to that special place where God rests and watches.

Our society doesn't teach balance. In fact, it teaches the opposite. It teaches our children to go out and to compete, to strive and push and pull, to buy this, acquire that, mortgage your life for a few bricks in the suburbs. We don't teach our children power and balance. We teach chasing a material dream. Girls are expected to be very sporty and to drink with the lads and compete not only on the sporting field, but sexually, in careers, financially, and so on. That's where happiness lies, we are told, but all of that makes for a hollow shell of a person. And that hollow shell and its insecurity has to be filled with something, be it drugs, alcohol, or dependencies of one kind or another.

If a woman gets too caught up in all this sort of biff bang, external world stuff, she loses herself, her spirituality, her sixth-sense perception, and she becomes numb. In trying to keep the ego happy, she spoils her sensitivity. Because it's in the quietness and softness that you become sensitive.

You will know, if you are a female, whether you have a balance around you, in your yin and yang energy, You will know when you are imbalanced, whether you are pushing too hard, trying too hard, becoming too much of a workaholic, buying too much of the ego's vision. Then perhaps you might be balanced the other way, if you have allowed softness and quietness to become too much a part of your life. So you are so soft and so quiet, you are unable to take action. Or perhaps you are too scared to go out into the marketplace so you can't sustain yourself at an economic level that will allow you to survive without much stress. There's a balance between polarities, and perception shows you where that balance exists.

On the **male** side of the equation, the physical body of a male and his psychology have a positive alignment—a tendency to go outward, the male ejaculates outward. He seeks for his goals outward, he goes outside of himself to seek his quest, his status in life, his position. He needs that outgoing energy to confirm himself as being solid and real. He needs competition, so he will be drawn toward sports. He needs people to observe him winning. He needs to be observed as clever, exercising his intellect. And he has to go out there to conquer the world, sexually or financially or in any manner, so that he can discover who he is.

A man feels he has power and identity through what he does. A female's identity is more aligned to what she feels.

Conversely, to the outgoing male energy, a man's spirituality is inner; it is in fact yin. It is very inward and it pulls in. So men are very secretive about what they believe. They're very secretive about their feelings. For the most part, it would seem that they don't have any feelings. They're just a product of thinking.

Men in our Western societies do not discuss their inner self and their emotions. It's not considered appropriate. They keep it all hidden away and secretive. The man's inner spirituality is on the negative polarity pulling in, while his external physical social self is yang, on the positive polarity pushing out. A metaphysical question develops in the male. The physical energy of the male pushing outward becomes separated from his spiritual energy within, that is pulling inward.

A male's perception, his sixth-sense sensitivity lies in balancing the gap. Most men because they are out there in life performing, attempting to establish observers, for they feel that that will make them solid, in fact create a big hole inside of themselves. For that outgoing energy pulls them away from softness and spirituality in the sixth sense. The outgoing striving nature of masculinity pulls the male away from his real power, his inner spiritual self.

Remember this, all extrasensory perception comes in softness and silence. A man who is out there biff banging along, achieving, ejaculating, and conquering will tend to lose the softness that he has. He may win medals in the external ego world, but in the meantime, he decapitates himself and goes blind in the etheric world, the inner world. It's only in softness and inward concentration that his real power flows.

Most men feeling the huge gap inside of themselves start to wonder who they are. And in all that worldly activity, they still never discover who they are. The way a man discovers who he is, is by gradually pulling back from the ego's world, from action, and disciplining himself. Now that might involve nutritional discipline, a period of celibacy, or time saved for putting his life in order after years of being out there campaigning. It might involve time to settle his paperwork and debts, to take stock of where he finds himself. And maybe he needs to get rid of encumbrances that are superfluous to his day-to-day needs.

He needs to acknowledge his spirituality and claim his true power. For the male, that is vital. He has to acknowledge his softness, and he has to get into a dialogue with his inner self. The easiest way to do that is through meditation, prayer, and contemplation. A male can communicate with God by simply sitting in a chair and thinking. If he is thinking objectively, and he's not conning himself, he can look at his strengths and his weaknesses. He can look within and see what works for him and what doesn't. He can begin to express that spirituality that is within him.

If you are male, make it a discipline to express that spirituality once a day to somebody. It could be an act of caring, a soft remark, a kind gesture. It might be picking up a child and holding it in your arms. It might be putting your arms around an old person and walking across the street with them. It's an affirmation that says that you are there as a sensitive and soft person and that you will allow that sensitivity to come out from your heart. I think that's a very important part of the balance of masculinity—to pull back from that natural male competitiveness and to allow the God force to come out from within, through softness and caring.

Of course, when you get into a male-female relationship, the female can assist the man spirituality to come out. He in turn can show her the strengths of the external yang, and he can protect her somewhat on an energy level, so that she can become more confident in the light of the masculinity around her. There's a balance, and it's important to stay inside that balance.

If, as a female, you become too masculine and competitive, you'll boom that energy out and often that will result in pulling to you a very wimpy type of guy, because wimpy guys are attracted to very positive, powerful masculine women. The wimp is looking for a mother to replace the one he lost when he became an adult. Therefore, the overly pushy woman is attractive to him for she won't require much of him. He won't have to become a John Wayne protective type.

A woman can be very spiritual and feminine and still be strong. Her femininity expressed outward is lovely, and it will attract a stronger sort of guy, because it's only a strong male who would be attracted to that kind of feminine softness. For now he can't play the little boy, he has to be a mature adult.

A woman needs a sensitive male she can talk to who isn't going to be there necessarily to fix all her stuff for her but who will be there to relate and understand when the female has emotional aspects of a journey to discuss that deal with subtlety of feelings. So the possibility of that yin and yang polarity is there in your relationship to give you power. It's important that you don't trash your balance so badly that you lose sight of the lightness of being.

The male also needs his balance. Because if he is too egotistical, too pushy, he's boring, isn't he? He just becomes the boasting jock who's constantly ejaculating his energy out seeking observers and admirers, the spiritual male that has embraced his sixth sense, is more in control, he's not scared of softness, and he can relate to his emotions and communicate his feelings properly.

Understand Your Shadow Self

As you develop perception, and open up to the sixth sense, and as you begin to comprehend the etheric, you also have to look at the psychological polarity in your life, the interaction of the dark and the light. As a part of understanding polarity, you have to work on your darker side, what Carl Jung called the shadow. It's a vital part in the development of the sixth sense, and one that is often overlooked.

Here's how it pans out. When you go deeper and deeper within yourself, as you open up your perceptions and your life and your chakras, you begin to straddle dimensions, and you perceive things that no one else perceives. In doing so, you place yourself in a wonderful, but mysterious world that is most immediate, where even the slightest, most obscure feelings you have inside of you may be manifest in front of you.

Each of us is the product of a million aspects, or bits of memory within. Many of those bits of yourself, you may not be aware of, as they lie very deeply hidden in your subconscious. You don't want the dark energy finding you at a vulnerable moment. And suddenly that manifestation of your dark side tries to bite you on the bum. So let's talk about how to handle it properly, and how to release it so it doesn't cause trouble.

Here's how we understand it in the light of the sixth sense. Even though you may be a very reasonable person and you may be good and operate well within society, within your family, deep within, the shadow is always there. We all have it because we are fragile humans. We have fears, antagonisms, and destructive tendencies that come not only from our family of origin and upbringing, but also from the sense of insecurity that comes from just being a human.

Think about how many disasters you have to avoid on an average day just to make it. There are many predators in society, and you have to stay balanced in order to stay well.

Jung, who made a great study of the shadow self, said that at any time you repress your shadow, it comes back to haunt you at a later date. So part of you getting in touch with all things is getting in touch with a shadow self, and that is a matter of going deep within. You can work with a therapist or on your own. But you have to look at the hatreds, the fears, the resentments, the anger that may reside within you. These emotions may be quite subtle, but in that subtlety you discover yourself.

A lot of people, for example, have a unexpressed anger and rage that manifests in their life, sometimes subtly, and they destroy their potential for success. They will often subtly obstruct others from reaching their goals. It's like the brat within. When the brat is out of control, it needs attention. It wants to make sure that no one is happy, and no one's doing well. By going within and looking for those shadow feelings, one sees that there is darkness inside all of us.

For me, it came as a dark night of the soul to see my shadow person so close up. It was rather disconcerting. You can so easily kid yourself that the social self you express in your interpersonal relationships, business, and family reflects the total of what you are, and it's easy to kid yourself what a good person you are, all sweetness and light and sugar and honey.

When I first came into contact with my shadow side, my reaction was one of regret and sadness, for I saw how the shadow within me was as yet unresolved, and I was most concerned. I remember thinking, I would not want to die and then enter the next world without having first resolved the negative part of my shadow. I realized how spiritually ugly it was and how much of it still remained inside of me. I felt an urgent need to attend to it—to birth the spiritual being and to reach the God force.

To bring out all of the sixth sense in its most glorious form, the shadow eventually has to be accommodated. It's usually done in meditation, silence, and serenity. You look for your hatreds, antagonisms, and fears, and you notice the emotional, mental, or physical violence that you express, and you accommodate the dark side by discovering how they all came about. Then you forgive yourself and you project love and compassion in directions where previously you projected negativity and nastiness. More often than not, your prejudices were taught to you by your family.

A child mimics its parents' insecurities, or it may learn hatred and envy from siblings or schoolmates. We are all taught to harbor resentments. It's part of our programming as children. For some, that antagonism may manifest as aggression and/or literally physical violence. For others, the violence is more covert. It's an emotional violence, a manipulation, that wielding of emotional power using disquiet or threats to control others. Perhaps the violence is verbal, abusive, sarcastic, cynical, or it depreciates others with a negative attitude.

Sometimes the shadow is nothing more than aggression, where you're walking along and pushing against people saying, *Out of my way, out of my way, I am off to conquer the world and get noticed. Out of my way.* If you are stepping on people to keep your ego happy, that aggression is a manifestation of the dark side of self. It too has to be accommodated and looked at as you process it out of your system.

Action Step: You can use various rituals to release the dark side. One of the techniques is to write down some of your darker elements or events in your life on a piece of paper, Then you can meditate upon them in a sacred way. Let's say next time you are with friends around a campfire, light that piece of paper, burning it, and say, *I return back to the God force these darker aspects of myself that I have now understood and processed. As I am now coming from my higher infinite self, please help me reconcile the dark and the light within me. In the end, we're all a mixture of both light and dark, love and hatred.*

The light has to be surrounded by the dark in order for it to shine. Dark complements light and allows the light to become special. In handling your shadow side, you release the need to project it on others, no longer making others a scapegoat for your inner disquiet. Much of the ills of our society are manifestations of people's shadows projected on others. Fascism and the rise of the Nazi Party in the 1930s was the outcropping of a nation's unresolved shadow made manifest in horrendous political and military events. Because our shadow self is very deep within, it feels foreign to us. It doesn't feel like it's a part of us. Therefore, we tend to project it outward toward organizations or people that feel different—toward anyone who seems foreign to us.

In this context, the American shadow is often projected on the African Americans, and they take the brunt of America's negative disquiet. In turn, the African Americans project their shadow on White Americans, seeing them as the bogeyman. It's a part of human psychology. There is no right and wrong of it, but the situation just needs resolving in a loving, compassionate way.

Until it is resolved, we will always try to find someone on which to park our shadow self. Sometimes we do it inside our families. In a family where there are several children, you will often find that one child silently agrees to become the shadow, and the rest of the family project their stuff onto that child. For example, Child A is all sweetness and light, and Child B is bright and helpful and sugar and spice. But Child C is a nightmare—

scream, rotate your head, spew green slime, that kind of stuff. Child C is the brat, the troublemaker, the unreliable one, the moody one, the one that we can blame and project our shadow upon.

We all create our shadow bogeymen, and they are either in our families or in our local society, or in our nations. In order to reach the quintessence of energy within us, in order to really understand who we are, we have to look at that shadow side. That may mean beating up on some pillows to release your anger. Or it may mean discovering how your insecurities and hatreds came about, and seeing that they are not real, that there are just things that you learned in childhood.

You can't blame yourself for your shadow side. The only blame occurs when you express it destructively, or you project it unreasonably upon others.

Once you acknowledge the negative part of the shadow inside of you, you accommodate it. You understand that it may have been a part of your innermost psychology, but it does not necessarily have to be a part of your life. You can choose and embrace lightness and good because you have accommodated your shadow rather than repressing it.

Now the shadow has a positive side, and I will explain. Many people think that the very word *shadow* implies the negative or dark, but the positive side of the shadow is where your deeper creativity lies. In there are talents and aspects that are hidden in your subconscious, The shadow, after all, is just a way of describing the unseen part of your memory.

Also in the positive side of your shadow is, I believe, the memory of your spiritual heritage, the fact that you are a being of light, an angel inside a human body, and that you have come from a spiritual dimension to be here on Earth, to learn and grow and interact with others in a loving way and eventually to go beyond the negative nature of this Earth experience, to embrace and return once more to the light. For in the shadow is your connection to the divine, to the nature self, to the spirits of earth, air, fire, and water and, of course, the fifth element, ether, or the etheric. Also in the positive shadow is all the extrasensory knowledge you already know and the doorway to the rest that you are still developing and bringing forward.

In the process of going inward, and looking and seeing, you discover stuff you never knew was in there. I found music in my shadow. I can't sing at all, and I don't play any instruments. But I found I could hear music with my feelings. So I engage my feelings to listen, rather than using a musical ear.

I have written eleven books, so far, and I have learned how to place words together. I found I could hang words off musical notes, even though I didn't know what the note was called, or where it was supposed to be. I became a songwriter and record producer. The first record I produced and wrote was called *Voice of the Feminine Spirit*. I made it with a Norwegian soprano called Cecilia. It was made for the New Age market. And it was an instant success selling over 100,000 copies, which in the New Age is close to miraculous.

Next, I wrote a kind of New Age opera with the flute player, Tim Wheater. It's called *Heart Land* and it's bit like a New Age Wagner. Music and producing records has given me a whole new place to play.

You never know what ideas and talents and opportunities lurk in the shadow once you start to look at it. Take the lid off and at first perhaps what you see is crud. And under the crud, maybe there is a Grammy or an Oscar, or a wonderful new creativity that may translate into a whole pile of money. Don't be scared of the shadow. It's okay.

If you have a chance, read Robert Johnson's book on the shadow: *Owning Your Own Shadow: Understanding the Dark Side of the Psyche*. This short book will help you grip the idea of the shadow self. Once you have cleared out the shadow, you step from darkness to light, from ignorance to the sixth sense. It's a part of the sacred journey. But you have to dump the hostility and the negativity of the shadow to scoop the good stuff, the creativity, and love and compassion that is also there—your spiritual self.

In your prayers and meditations and spiritual practices, process and bring out your shadow and release the negative and enhance the positive, creative side of self. Your perception grows out of compassion for yourself and others. The more you turn inward, and lovingly accept yourself, the more your mind and your emotions become clear and strong and purposeful.

And so the sixth sense comes through in an uncluttered way. It's automatic. In fact, you could say that the sixth sense comes from the clearing out of various aspects of self and the accepting of new values, as much as acquiring new perceptions and techniques.

About the Author

Thought to be one of the most renowned metaphysical teachers, Stuart Wilde described the etheric life-field around humans in precise detail in the 1980s. Among his many teachings about love and peace were his revelations about spiritual evolution, personal development insights, philosophies about where human beings really came from, and predictions about world events yet to come that he would regularly see in transcendental meditation. Throughout the course of Wilde's life, hundreds of his predictions came true.

Wilde was born in England and educated at St. George's College, Weybridge, Surrey. He joined the English Stage Company in Sloane Square, London. And he opened a jeans business in Carnaby Street London during the heyday of the 1960s.

He studied alternative religions and Taoist philosophy. He immigrated to the US and lived in California.

In the 1990s he toured regularly with Deepak Chopra, Dr. Wayne Dyer, and Louise Hay and lectured in New Thought churches and at New Age conferences.

He wrote more than twenty books—which were translated into twenty-seven languages and sold millions of copies worldwide—on the subjects of spirituality and personal development. He later executive produced and was the lyricist on popular New Age music albums.

In the course of his more than thirty years of teaching, Wilde appeared on hundreds of television shows and thousands of radio programs.

Wilde died in 2013 at the age of sixty-six. "Life was never meant to be a struggle; just a gentle progression from one point to another, much like walking through a valley on a sunny day," he said.

For more information: www.StuartWilde.com.